Shut Up and Sell!

Shut Up and Sell!

TESTED TECHNIQUES
FOR CLOSING THE SALE

Don Sheehan

Foreword by Norman Vincent Peale

amacom

American Management Associations

*This book is available at a special
discount when ordered in bulk quantities.
For information, contact Special Sales Department,
American Management Associations, Publications Group,
135 West 50th Street, New York, NY 10020.*

Library of Congress Cataloging in Publication Data

Sheehan, Don.
  Shut up and sell!

  Bibliography: p.
  Includes index.
  1. Selling.   I. Title.
HF5438.25.S477   658.8'.5   81-66235
ISBN 0-8144-5705-3   AACR2
ISBN 0-8144-7615-5 pbk

Printing number

10 9 8 7 6 5

This book would not have been possible
without the kind help and encouragement of
Reverend John O'Toole
Euclid, Minnesota

Foreword

NORMAN VINCENT PEALE

The title of this book, *Shut Up and Sell!*, gives the impression that it is written for salespeople. And it is, but it is also for any person who wants to win—who wants to do his job better, whatever it is.

An employer once told me he intended to fire a man from his job. "Why not fire him into the job?" I asked. "Why not build a fire within his mind?"

"How?" he asked.

"Get him to read a good, motivational, self-help book," I replied. He did, and a big fire was built in the man. He became an invaluable employee.

Had Don Sheehan's *Shut Up and Sell!* been available at the time, I would have recommended it for this desultory employee for a "fire builder." I know, for reading the book in manuscript has fanned up a fire in me. It made me want to do a better job of "selling" the Gospel and positive thinking.

This book will, for a fact, get a new enthusiasm going in your mind.

Don Sheehan's book is filled with down-to-earth, commonsense know-how about becoming successful in life. He sounds the trumpet calls and restates the tried and true attitudes that have historically summoned men and women to the top and which still point the way up.

But this book is not a wordy, inspirational document. The inspiration comes through specific, detailed, step-by-step suggestions on how to do it right. This is a true learning book by a teacher who knows how to teach. You become excited as you realize that a tough job can indeed be done successfully when you know how to do it right. And Sheehan outlines workable procedures that lead to success.

Shut Up and Sell! is a rare combination of motivation, inspiration, know-how, and common sense. It underscores the basic elements of desire and determination, of enthusiasm and positive thinking.

All told, it's one of the best guides to real success that I've read in a long time.

Contents

1
Portrait of a Closer

Who are the closers? The top closers make their sales because closing is never out of their minds. All through their interviews, they are conscious of the big secret: Think Closing! This hallmark of great closers separates them from ordinary salespeople. Top closers, both men and women, always think closing! The low closers never think that far ahead.

Three things are important: asking for the order, making the sale, and *closing*. Without this triple threat, you are just baying at the moon. Good closers are made, not born! Top closers know more, do more. They are professionals. They learn to use proper techniques. They develop timing, they know how to tailor-make closes. They learn and use enough closes to raise the odds in their favor. Good closers know they must be flexible, be able to make continuous adjustments. They can stop, restart, and try to close all over again. They are opportunists who spot places to close, then jump in and do their job. They believe in their methods of closing. Like scientists, they test their closing methods in the field. Techniques that get orders, they use and use. They constantly learn by studying reactions to their techniques so they can add to their sales arsenals. They buy books, tapes, and records and attend live seminars just to learn one new close, or to adapt another close. Good closers put their intelligence to work. They size up people. They can trust their own judgment.

You must test and use this material so your income will go up. You must use effort to get new ideas going. You must develop sharpness and alertness to be ready when your opportunity comes to close. You must be 100 percent awake if you want to earn more closes. You must have yourself "up" for every close, and then you'll close more. You must be eager to sell, ready to close. You must live to close.

You must be in control of the sale. You must keep yourself and the customer "on track to close." Don't allow the prospect—or yourself—to wander off that closing path. Be forceful—even ruthless! Keep the sale "locked on." Closing is "the road to glory" for both salesman and prospect.

Use instructional closes. Sometimes you literally show your prospect how he can get results by using your service or product.

Think of it: just one extra close per week means 50 extra closes per year—with two weeks off to gear up for more closings!

Look for your prospect's "hot button." Is he greedy for profits? Does he love recognition? Does he fear the loss of something if he does not buy?

Press hard on what you think will move your prospect to action. It's your "judgment play."

Lean on him a little harder. Remain in charge at all times. Keep pressing. Don't let up. Stay alert for spot buying signals. Step up your effort to move in fast for a close when you hear or see a strong buying signal. When you hear "your prices are higher than your competitor," it's 99 to one that the prospect wants your product. So don't defend your product, close instead! When people talk price, it means they're "hot."

Learn to negotiate, to debate, to handle details, to dicker, to keep up your momentum, to handle complaints with a quick "yes" while pointing out much stronger aspects of the product. Learn to be able to read your customer's behavior, facial reactions, and moods. Study him. Keep your presentation moving along to a climax. Don't defend your product. Be on the offensive all the time. Very likely, your best offense is your silence. If you do not say anything, the chances are your prospect will think his objection is too silly to talk about.

Use "test closes." "Shall I send this to you next week?" or "Do you think you'll need our new adaptor?" or "Will your board of directors appreciate your aggressiveness in this decision?" All you're doing is testing his conviction. These questions may not make him close, but at least they get you closer to a sale.

Don't get so grooved into your presentation—your "talkathon"—that you can't stop and close at any time. I repeat: be able to close at any point in your presentation— even with your opening statement. Anything you say after your prospect is ready to buy is a waste of words. Pride yourself on closing quickly.

Your key to more business is a three-letter word: "Ask!" Ask for the order, expect the order. You can almost demand an order. Even on a test basis, asking starts the ball rolling. It's right in the Bible: "Ask and you shall receive." To start building your repertory of closing statements, try: "We guarantee same-week delivery," "We guarantee same-week service," "My product will save you money," "My equipment will give you less downtime," "This merchandise is put in on 60-day consignment," "You don't gamble a dime!" "If it doesn't sell, you can return the unsold merchandise."

Don't lose patience with a customer, don't act frustrated,

keep your cool, don't look down on a prospect for not making a decision. You'll only turn him off. Keep your tolerance and patience with today's buyer if you want him to be tomorrow's customer.

2
Why Salespeople Don't Close

If you do not close most of your sales, you are part of a crowd. I almost said, "You are in good company," but you are really in bad company. You and far too many others have puzzled sales trainers for over 70 years. If you are not closing your sales, it could be because you fear a resounding "no." More likely you never sat down to do the step-by-step job of learning the basics of closing.

Preparation is a number-one basic. If you have an hour to work out a sales task, you should use 50 minutes to put together your closing statement and the strategy you need to close. Too many sales managers and salespersons spend almost all their preparation time on sales talks and barely any on closing. Your sales preparation could even mean practicing silence, learning to shut up. Too many salesmen overkill with talk.

What you want is a complete sales interview. You need a real bundle of closing. The more closing tricks at your command, the more you fire up your confidence. You become a real seller. In plain English, you develop the guts to ask for the order!

You also need a real hunger to close. In fact, you have to be hungry! My own observation—beefed up by the "amens" of managers taking my courses—is that 50 percent of your motivation dies when your spouse works. "My wife or husband brings home half the bread, so I can relax." You may object: "But we run our own business together, and I work hard!" Fine. Then you've got to motivate each other or kick each other in the hind end.

Persistence is another important closing ingredient. Jerry Blosalk of Chicago accounts for a major share of the success of Plywood, Minnesota, a real growth company. He organized files of prospects whom he phones for extra business. "Sometimes the time isn't right for a buyer to buy, so I call back, usually with excellent results." Jerry Blosalk closes his sales because he takes time and trouble to get back to his prospects. In other words, no follow-up, no close. When you fail to follow-up, you rob yourself and your company of from 30 to 50 percent of additional business.

Often it is not your fault when you "sell and sell" but never close. Your company may have told you to "learn the business for the first three or four months." You were not taught that you must learn to close. You fell for the easy way of "just learning the basics of selling." Your sales manager was not straightforward with you. He should have told you: "The first duty of a salesman is to attempt to close, find a close, or just plain get the business!" A good sales manager would have warned you that your sales pitch may be the ammunition but that, like a good hunter, you don't spray it all over the place.

Whether you, the salesman, are selling computers to the Arabs or jet engines to Israel, your job is to fire up the prospect, to make your buyer want action. You must understand that a large percent of everything sold in this world is bought on an emotional basis. To make the big sales, you must turn up the fire of desire in your customer's eyes. You must be fired up about what you are selling, and, for heaven's sake, don't let cold water put out your fire. The cold water of the closing game is the fear of failing to close.

John Loffler of Franklin Park, Illinois, says: "Salesmen have to be sold on the fact that they are important, and resold again."

3

Closing Is the Tip
of the Iceberg

Too many salespeople seem to think that a closing springs up
fully developed like Venus out of the bath. The story about
Venus is a myth. So is the idea that you can close deals
without preparing in advance. The closing is just the tip of the
iceberg, but it is solid, visible proof of the huge mass of
preparation your client does not see.

A good closer is the grown-up version of the boy scout.
He is now a buck scout. The good closer is not necessarily
greedy. In fact, he or she usually is not avaricious but is smart
enough to leave something on the table for the customer. The
good closer does know, however, that if he is going to put
meat on his own table, he has to hunt the most elusive buck of
all, the "almighty dollar." He—like any good operator—does
not pass the buck. He wants the buck to stop with him—
nicely nestled in his bank.

The buck scout even improves on the motto of his
younger counterpart, "Be prepared." The buck scout adopts
the motto "Be superprepared." He knows that you have to get

ready to close before your customer gets ready to fight back. He knows that plotting is better than rotting. He knows that a lot of salesmen are rotting in waiting rooms because they did not get ready to close.

You have to discipline yourself in closing. You must eat right, sleep right, and think right to *train yourself to be a great closer*.

Some years ago, Ralph Cardoza of Cardoza Furniture Store in St. Paul told me he always asks his people to "get an extra hour of sleep the night before a big sale." His suggestion amazed me. I experimented with it and found that it works! Now, I deliberately teach people to use this great rule, because I've found—and so have thousands of others—that extra sleep cuts down your irritability. When you get that extra sleep, you tend to be more patient and more tolerant, and you try to please. Your closing percentage always goes up when you're rested!

I'm also thankful to Rudy Boschowitz for his suggestion: "You must give more to customers in time and help if you are to sell more." You just cannot do this if you're not rested. This can mean six to eight hours of sleep.

Discipline in closing calls for a good amount of mental regimentation in your closing efforts. How should you handle the prospects? Should you start with a close right off? Should you wait to detect strong buying signals? Should you let the prospect sell himself? The disciplined professional is always analyzing his chances for a close by being alert. He is an opportunist: he's ready to win. He knows more closes, tries to close more often—and does close more often.

My experience tells me that 50 percent of all sales are closed directly *after the presentation by almost mutual consent*. Make sure you project yourself well. Too many salespeople are too sensitive or too emphatic. The better salespeople use their will to overpower the prospect.

To close a sale, the professional uses five or more different closes to get the job done. The average salesman knows two closes but uses only one close on everyone. He gives everyone the same old close, and then he wonders why selling hasn't paid him much. He needs to learn by heart— yes, memorize—six to eight different closes for different types of prospects and situations. He thus adds strength and variety to his closing plan. Otherwise, he's like a man using just one leg to swim, forgetting he has two hands, a chest, a head, and another leg. Mark Spitz would have been lucky to win a lead medal if he swam like that. Selling in today's world is like competing all the time in the Olympics. You need all the closings you can get.

Before we even discuss closing technique, it is urgent that we discuss buying signals, both oral and physical. As a sales trainer, I define buying signals as "anything a prospect does, or says, that could signal—to the alert salesman—that the prospect has a deep interest in buying." You should be alerted by: "How much does it cost?" "When can I get delivery?" "What do you think, dear?" "Can I get terms—pay for it, say, in three payments?" "How long is your warranty?" "How much of a down payment is necessary?" You must listen to the prospect to determine if he has mentally purchased the product or the service.

Physically, he may rub his chin, fold and unfold his hands, pace up and down, ask for directions to the bathroom, pick up the item or the literature. These may be physical signs that your prospect is satisfied. The time is now ripe to ask closing questions. You saw the signals, and one of them was the green light that said, "Go!" The oral or physical buying signal is your traffic sign. If you can't "read" the green signal, you will be left at the curb.

It is crucial to set the right scene for a close. Whether you are in a consumer's home, a prospect's office, or on a showroom floor, the proper setting is important!

In a home, have candy, gum, or something for the small children. Ask permission from the mother to give your gift to the children. You must also get that TV set turned off as fast as you can. Get the husband and wife in front of you—otherwise they signal to each other.

In an office, try to get the door closed. Ask permission: "Do you mind if I close the door?" If the telephone rings while you are in your presentation, wait until your prospect finishes the call. Then say, "My talk will take another four minutes. I'd be most appreciative if you could ask your secretary to hold all calls for the next four minutes. Thank you." The next step is to surprise your prospect by finishing in three minutes! Your brevity could make the difference! When you're in a prospect's office, do not sit directly across from him. If possible, sit at the side of his desk. He then has to turn his attention to you instead of fiddling with papers or objects on his desk. Play him as you would a trophy fish. When he sits down, you stand up. This gives you a slight psychological advantage. You look down at him—not figuratively, but from a standing position.

TEN FAULTS THAT ANNOY BUYERS

1. Overtalking. Allow your prospect to talk—he may talk himself into buying.
2. Interrupting. Your customer could be right in the middle of his acceptance speech.
3. Being poorly dressed. Nice shirts, spruce ties, pressed pants, and shined shoes are what you wore when you went courting.
4. Not listening. See "interrupting." Your client could be telling you he's ready to go and you don't hear him!
5. Scratching, burping, and the like.
6. Untidiness. If you've lost a button off your coat or shirt,

your customer might feel, "This guy is eating enough to pop his buttons, so he really doesn't need the business."

7. Gawking. While you are eyeing the bric-a-brac—especially personal things—on your prospect's desk, he could get the idea you are more interested in his golfing trophies than in his order.

8. Being disorganized. If you don't really know what you are doing, your customer knows he isn't going to get much help from you. In fact, he is not going to put your name in lights for wasting his time.

9. Uncleanliness. If you forget the old arm spray, your prospect may get the idea your deal smells too.

10. Insincerity. Flatter your customer and he might decide you are also flattering your product.

Put your ego in your pocket when selling. Try not to talk about yourself. Talk about your prospect or about people in your company who help you: your engineering staff, your shipping department, your delivery department, your manager. Put the spotlight on others. A true professional praises only others. If you or your product is really good, there will be plenty of people to sing your praises. You can applaud yourself until Doomsday, but you won't succeed until your audience starts clapping for you.

Take a hard, cold look at yourself. Do you warm people up to you, or are you turning people off? Are you fun to be with, or are you like an IRS man with a bad case of the gout? If anyone is going to take a good hard look at you, it had better be you and not your client who does it! If your self-appraisal tells you that you rival a wet fish, please do something about it! Remember what I said about rest!

Maybe a bit of relaxation will put a smile back on your face. I used to read P. G. Wodehouse when I got owly. Now I have enough Jeeves and Bertie Wooster stories in my mind to do the trick. I can look like a St. Bernard dog who has been sucking a lemon, but if I recall Bertie's description of one of his hangovers ("Jeeves, make that canary quit stamping around his cage with hobnailed boots!"), I light up with a smile. Winning the Irish Sweepstakes couldn't do much better!

It also helps to ask yourself some more pointed questions. They may make you feel uncomfortable, but if you are comfortable with your closing record, you can ignore them! Otherwise, do something about them!

1. Is my income what I want it to be?
2. Is my dress up to date? Do I have a "top" wardrobe?
3. Do I have a daily study period of at least 60 minutes?
4. Am I at or near the top in my company or industry?
5. Do I do what it takes to succeed?
6. Am I grooming myself for more opportunities?
7. Do I want to own my own business?

Now, if after these questions—these seven self-directed arrows—you have a few punctures in your complacency, I am thrilled. I can almost become poetic—along the lines of some dimly remembered doggerel:

> I shot some arrows in the air
> They lit I know just where!
> —In the false illusions of my pride!

As a salesman, how much better are you today than you were a year ago? Do you really believe in self-improvement through daily study? How many books have you read on salesmanship and motivation? If you are a top closer, it has to be 20 to 30 books.

How many tapes on selling did you listen to? Are you better dressed than a year ago? Is your weight the same or lower than a year ago? What are your future plans for self-improvement? It's as simple as falling off water skis! Either you are going up in selling, or you're coming down!

Are your selling skills up to date? Are you giving the same sales talk this year as you did last year? Is your closing average up or down?

How are your human relations skills? Are you able to get along well at home, at the office, with the customers? Do you organize or agonize?

Are you upgrading yourself in all these areas, or are you allowing yourself to skip some? In selling, you have three choices: drift, drown—or close.

Are you tough-minded enough? Are you getting ready for the 1980s by growing every month? Are you climbing upward, or are you stationary? Is your thinking on a higher level than a year ago?

To be a top closer, you need the three D's:

> Dedication to your product or service.
> Discipline so you don't fall apart at price resistance.
> Determination to sell at your prices and terms.

TEN CLOSING "SPARKS"

1. *Review your personal goals.* Decide what do you want out of selling: trips, a lake home, or whatever. Then review your goals daily to build your determination to close.
2. *Keep a record of your closings.* What is your closing score? Not one salesman in 500 knows his closing average! Most salesmen actually do not know how many customers they saw to get a sale! Is it one in five? One in three? You'll never know until you keep a record of your closings!

3. *Practice, practice, practice.* Rehearse with yourself—or anyone who will listen—exactly how you will close.
4. *Expect a fight in closing.* Expect resistance. Plan for resistance. In fact, welcome resistance! It's the strongest buying signal you can possibly get!
5. *Expect to get your second wind during the highs and lows of the sales presentation.* Try to gain momentum in your favor, then act on it to close the sale quickly.
6. *Before the sale, review previous customer testimonial letters.* Testimonial letters not only help sell customers but also help salespeople sell themselves on their product or service. Reading good, strong testimonial letters on the merits of your product or service simply does a "good inside job on you."
7. *Keep your cool during the sale.* Do not show any emotions! If you are "up" or "down," don't show it. Like a good poker player, you don't call attention to yourself. You watch the other players. By controlling your emotions you ensure that you won't miss any physical or verbal buying signals. Control yourself, and you'll stay in control. If the client says, "Your prices are too high," do not show hostility. Just say, "Oh?" in an offhand way. If there were a shorter word, I would recommend it!
8. *Concentration builds determination.* As the sale proceeds, do not allow yourself to be distracted by other people, phones, interruptions. Keep 100 percent of your attention on the prospective buyer. Be relaxed yet alert.
9. *Be optimistic before, after, and during the sale.* Optimism is the very soul of salesmanship. It is telegraphed to the buyer. Optimism is the badge of the winner.
10. *Guard your determination.* Win, lose, or draw—but don't let anything knock you out for the next prospect. Above all, do not carry defeat to the next sale.

SHEEHAN'S TEN TOP RULES OF CLOSING

1. Prepare yourself, both mentally and physically, for closing the sale today.
2. Double-check dress.
3. Start to close at once.
4. Concentrate on closing.
5. Talk little, punt mostly.
6. Try five or six methods to close.
7. Prepare to get your second wind.
8. After asking a closing question, remain silent.
9. Stay ten minutes to an hour longer than usual.
10. Thank your prospect and exit quickly with the order.

SEVEN STEPS TO CLOSE

1. Analyze the market.
2. Prepare and organize.
3. Deliver the sales talk.
4. Close the sale.
5. Record the facts.
6. Service your client.
7. Promote or perish.

4

Set Fire to
Your Coattails

The top closers are the superstar salespeople. They've "learned to learn" quickly and are usually loners. They don't run with the pack; they do things differently. Superstar salespeople have made themselves experts in closing. They close often and easily. They usually have 110 percent dedication to their job. They prefer to create rather than compete. They are experts at self-organization—definitely not unorganized as you so often hear. Superstars are always studying. They buy books. They are the course-takers. They are very future-minded. They are the guys who set fire to their own coattails.

Instead of working and working, and being cut down by fatigue, the superstar uses his head as a fulcrum. An engineer needs a fulcrum for the lever that does the heavy work. He doesn't overwork; he knows where the breaking point is. The superstar, using his head as a fulcrum, has the leverage he needs to get the big jobs done without knocking himself out.

The superstar is a "buck smeller." He or she is motivated by money and doesn't mind admitting it.

Most people are motivated by praise, recognition, and other ego builders. The superstar already has a big ego. What makes him sell is that, in his view, he has chronic money problems. He is always in urgent need of money. This pushes him to sell more.

His ego is offended if he loses a sale. He may even secretly hate the prospect who makes him work so hard to gain a sale.

There are only three or four superstars in a thousand salespeople. They are, indeed, rare commodities, but there are enough of them in the country to keep the wheels of industry rolling. Your supersalesman is the great closer who keeps the economy going. He closes out old business and opens up the new.

Even in today's troubled economy, approximately 10 percent of all salespeople make $25,000 a year, but only 2 percent make $50,000! It's not unusual for our superstar to make $50,000 a year before the age of 30. Supersalespeople don't have to talk big; they *are* big!

If you have the desire to be "number one," don't feel bad about it or curse the "demon of ambition." I had this ambition for two nationally known companies, and I never regretted it the least bit.

What I'm saying is, make up your mind you're going to win every contest your company sponsors. Use all its tools to close on its specials, deals, and introductory offers. Believe in your company. Be prepared to work early and late. Use the company's contest to help spur you on. Get to bed earlier, eat right, plan right, use everything you've got to outsell, outfight your fellow company salesmen, your competition.

Be a glory hound, to be in the spotlight, to become a legend in your company—like invincible heroes out of the storybooks. Wear the best clothes and the all-American smile, to let them know you're unbeatable.

My Olympic coach told me when I was just 14: "It's year-round dedication that makes you a champion." Joe Collins was a quiet man, but he taught me that you "live to win." At least that was the message I learned from him after training under him for four years. My coach's inspiration helped me win in Canada when everyone else was supposed to do the winning.

If you've got ambition to sell, keep it alive every day by thinking of being number one. Look like a champion. Talk like a winner. Walk like you're going somewhere—and before you know it, you'll be there!

Do you have special qualities to "take it"—to take the rough with the smooth? Remember Rudyard Kipling's poem, "If you can keep your head when all about you are losing theirs and blaming it on you, if you can lose and start all over, if you can force yourself to continue, then you'll be a man, my son." Don't feel bad on hard-selling yourself after inevitable setbacks.

Can you endure? Can you take the turn-downs? The setbacks? Can you regroup your forces after these defeats and launch your own blitzkrieg offensive? Many a smashing offensive was triggered by setbacks.

This is a good spot to remind you of Robert Bruce and the spider. Remember? Bruce, thoroughly beaten by the English, was hiding out in a cave. While treating himself to a lot of fancy self-pity, his attention was attracted by a spider which was trying to get a strand of webbing across the cave entrance. The spider repeatedly failed, but he endlessly kept trying. Of course, the spider finally made it. That's always what happens when someone keeps trying.

Needless to say, the great Scottish leader came out of hiding, regathered his army, and whaled the bejabbers out of the English.

Few salesmen ever make big money in selling, simply because they lack the "killer instinct" to close. They don't have that extra something to pursue the close when the buyer is on the fence. The salesman must realize it's difficult for the buyer to make up his mind about anything, much less to buy something. The "killer instinct" has to be developed, kept sharp by the salesman. When the salesman keeps himself "lean, mean, and hungry," he'll stay in the top-closer frame of mind.

The biggest single problem of a salesman is basic day-in and day-out prospecting for new business. His second biggest problem is having enough guts to close.

The Chinese have a saying: "You don't eat unless you're hungry." The same is true in closing! Our American sales-people are usually well satiated with plenty to eat, good places to sleep, and lots of comforts. This is an extremely dangerous situation, because it sets them up to be only half successful. So management should constantly look to the future and jack up salespeople's wants. The salesman is even smart to do this to himself. I feel only 2 percent of all salesmen are self-starters, 23 percent need supervision to keep their momentum, and 75 percent need a boss!

If you get your goals up, you will bring up your closings. You match your closings to your desires.

Many American factory workers go home with $150 a week for 40 hours of work. A good salesman who wants to live decently should go home with a gross income of four times that, or $600 per week. That would give him an annual income of $30,000. Even $30,000 per year in these times of high inflation is not that much to rave about.

Incidentally, approximately 90 percent of our salesmen are on a combination pay plan—base salary plus commission. Only 10 percent are on straight commission. My recent tour of the United States told me that straight-commission sales-people tend to make more money. I believe more salespeople should have the option of going on straight commission. Many straight-commission salesmen tell me it's either "sell or be sold"—an interesting philosophy all by itself.

In my travels I have met hundreds of salespeople making big incomes who prefer straight-commission selling and seem to thrive on it.

Curt Hames of Cedar Rapids, Iowa, George Philips of Billings, Montana, Jack Bishop of Fergus Falls, Minnesota, and George O'Neil of Novato, California, are among the outstanding people who have championship sales records. They are straight-commission salesmen who only want the opportunity to sell! They don't want expense accounts, draws—just a chance to sell again and again! Only 2 percent of our salespeople are "born salesmen." The other 98 percent are made through trial and error and "mental sweat."

I've stood at the graveside of John F. Kennedy and read his words, "Ask not what your country can do for you. . . ." I worked for the widow of the great Dale Carnegie. I stood in admiration before Winston Churchill's statue in Parliament Square in London. I visited Florence, Italy, to gaze in wonder at Michelangelo's sixteen-foot statue of David. I've heard the cherished words of Bishop Fulton Sheen, "May God love you." I've hung on Dr. Norman Vincent Peale's words on the "power of positive thinking." I've watched Olympic coaches like Johnny Werket instill their philosophies in their hopeful team members. From all these great men comes the same theme of resolve—the insight that with determination you can put it all together and win. You gain new hope where there was despair.

The beauty of determination is that it works for "the low and the hopeful" as it does for "the high and the mighty."

The top closer knows that he must habitually be "psyched up" to close. He knows this frame of mind is necessary if he is going to get his share of the business out there in the hunting area. He'll deliberately sit down and use Dr. Hornel

Hart's "Auto Suggestion" on himself—a form of self-hypnotism that helps the top closer guarantee his sharpness, his total commitment to the closing. This form of self-hypnosis gives him the "edge" his competition either won't use or doesn't know how to use. Closing is truly an attitude of the mind, and the top closer has it.

The real closer develops, and must continually reactivate, this attitude of mind. He turns on the juice before a sale. It's a chain reaction that helps him stiffen his spine. His "pep talk" to himself helps the top closer do an "inside job" on himself. Then he wins the signed order that puts meat on the table.

The novice, or "greenie," will stroll into a sale without using the technique of "psyching himself up," and he will always be at a great disadvantage because he lacks the right kind of preparation. What knocks out the green salesman faster than anything is his lack of success at closing sales. He invariably blames himself and his products, and never completely understands that he has not "conditioned" himself to the tough job of getting orders signed on the dotted line. He tells his boss the reason the prospect didn't buy was because "our prices are too high." The real problem was he didn't sell!

A pro never asks a prospect to sign a contract. Instead, he asks him to "okay the agreement." The close, "Please okay the agreement," avoids the harsh words "sign" and "contract."

The pro expects a fight on getting an order and is not upset over resistance. The green salesman takes resistance personally. Use words like "investment" instead of "cost." Don't use words like "purchase" but "When you own this product."

Salesmen too often are fickle, moody, or even unreliable. They just sell in spurts. The real trick is to spurt and hold it—to spurt and stay spurting.

How do you do this? Take a tip I learned from Keith Dickenson of Montevideo, Minnesota. He prides himself on reading at least one book a week to keep his inspiration high. This is an excellent idea. I know from talking to hundreds of salespeople that the easy way to keep the momentum up is to read inspirational books.

The vast majority of salesmen condemn themselves to mediocre living mainly because they lack the inspiration to sell. They refuse to take the time to build a fire in—or under—themselves. The inspired salesman knows that if he is going to start fires in other people, he first has to start one in himself.

Mike Zafran of Hammond, Indiana, assembled some do-it-yourself furniture and then sold two sets while hardly anybody in the company was selling anything. He closed by "putting it together." Mike took the time to learn all about do-it-yourself furniture. This built his own confidence and enthusiasm. This feeling was conveyed to prospects, who quickly became purchasers. His fellow salesmen did not have the self-determination that Mike built up in himself. Mike built his own fire in himself, then in others. One burning match will ignite others when you get them close enough. Mike's self-confidence made his customer say: "By golly, if this guy can put this stuff together, so can I!"

The G.I. Bill was offered to more than 11 million service people. The government offered to pay for books, tuition, family support, and even a living allowance for trainees. Guess how many took advantage of this "free" education! 75 percent? 50 percent? 25 percent? The shocking truth is that, up to now, only 5 percent have taken advantage of this fantastic offer! I am one of the 5 percent; and, frankly, I made a fortune out of that extra schooling.

Think of it! Nearly 95 percent turned it down! Some felt they could do better on their own and did, but many condemned themselves to mediocrity.

The educated person who is motivated can easily make from $500,000 to $1 million more during his or her career than

people whose education is too slight or acquired too late. The
average college graduate will usually make $250,000 more
than the non-college person. Yet, strange as it seems, high
school graduates and people with one or two years of college
make the best salespeople. However, company owners and
managers who can combine management with sales work
usually fare much better than the "first plain salesman," and it
is usually the college training that makes the difference.

The best-known way to keep up "steady spurt" selling is
to keep educating yourself by reading books and attending
seminars.

TEN BOOKS FOR INSPIRATION

1. *The Magic of Thinking Big* by Dr. David Schwartz.
2. *Power of Positive Thinking* by Dr. Norman Vincent Peale.
3. *Think and Grow Rich* by Napoleon Hill.
4. *How to Live 365 Days a Year* by John A. Schindler, M.D.
5. *I Ain't Much Baby, But I'm All I've Got* by Dr. Jess Lahr.
6. *Psycho-cybernetics* by Dr. Maxwell Maltz.
7. *How to Win Friends and Influence People* by Dale Carnegie.
8. *How I Raised Myself from Failure to Success in Selling* by
   Frank Bettger.
9. *I'm OK, You're OK* by Thomas A. Harris, M.D.
10. *Type A, Type B* by Meyer Friedman, M.D.

These top books by top writers are all in paperback form.
Give this list to your bookstore, and let them hunt them
down. Incidentally, whether I'm in London, New York, San
Francisco, or Rome, I always hunt first for a bookstore. I ask
the clerk for the business, inspirational, and self-help book
section. I've picked up outstanding books all over the three
continents, and I've profited greatly. You too can profit by
getting the manager of your local bookstore to help you build

your own home library. It need not be big, but it will open up to you some big country—some new horizons!

IRS laws favor your buying of books and tapes, attending seminars, and using any of the many available training aids. These are all tax-deductible if purchased to increase your effectiveness.

The big point I want to make is this: you must get into the education business! Set up something better than the old one-room school: a one-student school in which you are both teacher and pupil.

You must buy more self-help and inspirational books if you are going to increase your Go Power, the drive you need to close faster, easier—and more often! When you fire up your inspiration on your own, you close! So, try me out for just 30 days in this reading suggestion. Drop me a letter on your progress—or problems. I'll try to help.

When you don't close, you lose—but it is worse to sit around feeling sorry for yourself. George N. Kaha said, "Discouragement is a luxury no salesman can afford." Hurry up and see another prospect so that the next time you can get closer to a close. In fact, don't cry! Create! Every call on a prospect is another chance for a close. Remember, you'll be outstanding if you close 20 to 25 percent of your customers right off the bat, right at that first interview.

Many sales take weeks, months, even years to "cook" or, if you prefer, "incubate." The persistence factor comes in here. Only 10 percent keep trying to close. In fact, the New York Sales Club survey shows that 48 percent of the salespeople quit after their second call; only 10 percent make four, five, or six calls. These 10 percent sell 60 percent of everything that's sold in the United States. What they are telling you, loud and clear, is: "Don't fold if you don't close a customer the first time!" Sit down and figure out your customer's total capacity to buy in the future. Could he or she spend $100,000 with you? A million? What is the customer's buying potential? Ask yourself, what is the life cycle of a customer?

When you lose a sale, don't show your disappointment. On the other hand, don't show your joy if you make the sale. The prospect may think there's something wrong with your product, otherwise why should you be so happy to unload it? The prospect won't admire you either if you show too much discouragement. This could be like saying: "Nobody wants to buy this crummy junk!" Just keep your cool. Don't be in selling just to "try it out."

The short-range salesperson seldom makes it. Be in selling forever! Be what I called "a Lifer." By being a "Lifer," you only have short-term setbacks. Discouragement has little or no effect on your total career. So if you have a bad week or month (who doesn't?), get right back to the business of selling and closing.

When you allow a lost sale to affect you, you automatically lessen your chance on the next call to close. When you're down, your enthusiasm is down, your ego is battered—and, whether you know it or not, your chances of closing are way, way down. Don't let your chin droop. Teach yourself to forget the failings of an hour ago, the disasters of yesterday. Train yourself to wipe your mental blackboard. Then think of victories. Soon "the sweet smell of success" will again entice you.

When you don't close—resist falling apart! Get to other prospects fast. Learn to forget your defeats and forget them fast! Discouragement is nothing more than a form of self-pity. When I returned home from Korea, where I had contracted malaria and lost 40 pounds, I told my mother that I felt like I was falling apart. She quickly turned to me and said, "Winners in life don't take time to fall apart—oh yes, by the way, son, on your way out, empty the garbage!" A fine way to welcome a returning serviceman! That good "kick in the pants" helped me plenty in life. My old Irish mother was a master at it. So if you don't close, don't feel sorry for yourself! Don't brood! Don't let it spoil your day! Just treat that little defeat with your left hand—the back of your left hand. That leaves your right hand free to greet the next prospect—with the firm grip of a winner!

Discouragement through rejection has to be the number-one cause of failure of men and women in sales. Salespeople worry about turn-downs even before they make their calls.

I was turned down by the governor of Minnesota, but I still got my request accepted! Why worry about turn-downs? There are hundreds of places all over the globe to get business. Don't limit yourself to just a small area. Expand to counties, states, overseas. Sales can be won all over the world.

A salesperson has only one life. To improve it, he or she needs these seven valuable ingredients.

1. A great determination to close.
2. Product knowledge.
3. Imagination.
4. Good human relations—24 hours a day at home and at work.
5. A system of getting new customers—12 months out of the year.
6. A sense of humor.
7. A desire to keep closing.

Despite a previous poor showing or sales losses, you can make more closes than ever before. You can become the comeback salesman of the year for your company! One year, when I ended up second in standings for the Carnegie Company, I vowed to Ollie Crom, Mrs. Dorothy Carnegie's son-in-law, that I'd be back next year as the number-one producer, worldwide. I worked night and day and never felt tired. In Boston I was awarded my fourth trophy for being the number-one producing salesman, worldwide. The band played the University of Minnesota "Rouser" as I proudly accepted my gold trophy. On my way back to my seat in the hall, hundreds of hands, smiles, voices, and flashbulbs filled my cup with happiness. All I could think of was how I had lost the year before and how glad I was that I had the determination to win. I had turned defeat into a burning desire to win!

Will you hang on? Will you stay in there and try to win? How much guts do you have?

Love, desire, money, sex, power, greed are all exciting words, but the most motivating word in the world is "dissatisfied." When your back is to the wall; when you've been turned down time after time; when you are "sick and tired of being sick and tired"—that's when you've reached the right degree of dissatisfaction. At that point you're eager to close that sale, because you're sick of losing. No detail is too big or too small for you. You're just sick and tired of taking second or third—or of not going anywhere at all!

It had to be a completely dissatisfied guy who said, "Problems are not obstacles but unsolved opportunities."

TEN EXCUSES FOR NOT CLOSING

1. "We are in a recession, so salesmen aren't closing." Well, don't throw gasoline on the fire by some more non-closings!
2. "It's just before tax time." So don't wait until tax time. Who has money to buy then?
3. "Not enough rain," or "too much rain." These excuses are known as "covering the waterfront."
4. "The Arabs and their oil embargo!" At this point a really good closer looks for some Arabs.

5. "It's too hot (or too cold)." If the weather is good, this excuse can be re-edited to: "It's too nice!"
6. "Just before the first of the month." This is a better excuse for the loser than the tax excuse. He can use it 12 times a year.
7. "Our prices are too high." So drop the prices and get profit margins down. This adds another excuse: "Our commissions are too low."
8. "My territory is too big (or too small)." What really is the problem is that the territory is in the wrong hands.
9. "Competition has a better product (or service)." This is a really great excuse. As many salesmen can use it as there are companies.
10. "Buyer is not in the mood." Boy, are you lucky! You can sell him before he gets in the mood and buys from any dumb-dumb!

It seems there's never a "right" time. You can rationalize and rationalize. These ten excuses are used by hundreds of salesmen every day. They are as worthless as the salesman who lives on tomorrow's promises: "See me next trip," "I'll buy this fall," or "Give me a call this spring." If you accept these put-offs, you've allowed your prospect to con himself into believing he'll buy next time. If you record this information in your call book, you just complete the vicious circle. Like two guys lost in the woods, the two of you go in circles. Take my word on it, you just don't sell a prospect if you let him put off until tomorrow what he should do today. Make a holy resolution now that you are going to do a better selling job on people by closing now. Anticipate objections. With respect to the man who wants to wait until fall, tell him it will cost him more in the fall, even before you ask him to buy. That is no lie! He is going to waste more of his valuable time listening to you again. (You know that, but don't let him know!)

Expect objections; plan for them. Then answer them before the prospect raises them. Try this and see how well you can avoid objections.

Don't tolerate stalls or put-offs. Act a bit impatient with the pussy-footing prospect to hurry the closing. A lot of prospects are like hot-air balloons. Get a bit of heat under them, and they get off the ground faster.

Stand your ground. Expect to fight for the close. Most prospects have plenty of trouble making up their minds. Expect them to want to put off any kind of a decision. The fault is not "in the stars" but in yourself. Stop excusing yourself for your failures. Don't blame others for your failing to make a sale. Most salesmen just "hope" to sell. Why not deliberately *try* to sell? Weak salesmen claim the "company doesn't advertise enough," "I called at the wrong time," or "The prospect I saw can't make a financial decision." Why not forget the excuses and call on the person who can make a financial decision on your product? You can come up with 1,000 reasons why prospects didn't buy, but there is really only one: you failed to sell them. You accepted the prospect's excuses, which were just his polite talk to get you out of there. You just wasted an interview, because there was not enough sell from start to finish.

Go back to selling! Forget about manufacturing excuses. Even good excuses don't pay commissions or expenses.

When your customers make excuses, you know they're weak-kneed and can't make a decision. If they are people of action, people who can make up their minds, they don't need excuses. They either say yes or throw you out on your ear!

5
How Should a Salesman Dress?

The question is often asked: "Should I wear a one-piece suit?" I hear the question asked all over the country. You may have answered the question for yourself, but in case you have not, let me help you.

First of all, people want to deal with a person who is business all the way. Women have more leeway than men in the way of dress, but even they must use good taste—and good sense. For a male the problem of good judgment is even greater. The average salesman deals with people whose dress is dictated by their occupation—blue-collar workers, farmers, nurses, or others who wear uniforms. Just as you expect your prospect to be dressed as he is because of what he does, your client expects you to be dressed according to the role you play: as a person engaged in the business of selling—and with the accent on business. Men without ties or salespeople who take on the coloring of a peacock distract rather than attract.

You can quickly rule out red-and-green sport coats, beads

around your neck, turtleneck sweaters, and leisure suits. Although more than half the people you deal with are under 30, another 20 percent are over 65. Why take the chance of offending any age group? In 25 years as a trainer of salesmen I have never heard of anyone being criticized because he was wearing a business suit. When we ask people to shell out thousands or even more for our products or services, we had better look the part of people on whom our customers can rely. If you dress too casually, your client may get the idea that the thing you are good at is not business but pleasure.

Your overall appearance should not suggest a dude, a playboy, or a loafer.

Wear boots, wing tips, or any other style of shoe—but please, no patent leather! Your footwear should be polished daily. Your shirts should be white or blue, and your socks ought to be blue or brown.

Hair is again being worn shorter and neater all over the country.

Personal grooming—clean fingernails, a fresh, clean smell, tasteful accessories—is still the mark of a champion. The superstars in the world of selling neglect no detail: effective body deodorant, an attractive billfold, a well-pressed suit, a fresh, booze-free breath. They stand head and shoulders over the salespeople of 20 years ago, who were voted slobs of the nation by most everyone.

A few minutes a day is enough to select the tasteful apparel that is the benchmark of the professional. The wheels of commerce will be made to roll faster by a truly professional sales force. You must make yourself responsible for putting at least one professional-looking salesman in the public eye. In addition to yourself, you must add your people to that elite group made up of men and women who look smart because they are smart.

Without speaking a word we drive people away from our

sales centers because of outlandish dress. If you do not believe this, ask yourself how often you have been tempted to pick up a scraggly, long-haired hitch-hiker. Even the wearing of leisure suits at conventions is out of order.

Clothes may not make the man, but they do improve him. So forget the leisure suit when you are working. If one of your salesmen insists on wearing a leisure suit, quickly give him the chance to be consistent. Swiftly and firmly cut him from your sales staff so he can practice full-time leisure. If he protests, just explain: "Look, friend, better you should go into full-time leisure than have both of us on relief—and that is just what is going to happen if I have to earn enough for both of us!"

You do not want to look like a rainbow—and please, no dark glasses! They disturb prospects. High-heeled shoes are in the same category.

Dress the part! Don't feel you are ever overdressed. The prospect will believe what he sees. If you have the prosperous look, he will take you for what you are: a moneymaker. The buyer should also see that you are making money because you do a top job for everyone—your company and your customer.

Look like a winner and you'll feel like a winner.

According to a very good authority, you should have these items in your clothes closet:

3 winter suits.
3 summer suits.
3 coats for summer, winter, and in-between seasons.
5 pairs of shoes for all seasons.
5 white shirts.
3 blue shirts.

You can expect to have a $2,000 to $3,000 wardrobe investment. It's part of the price you pay to win. It is an investment. For you it is the hottest buy on the market.

6
Save Words, Make Dollars

When you sell, don't teach or tell—sell! After I taught a class of 50 salespeople this idea in Omaha, one cold January day, Tom Gartner, owner of Gartner Home Sales, told me that Teach, Tell, or Sell made a lot of sense. "We had salespeople who were just town criers. All they did was tell people about our houses."

The tell-type salesman really isn't sold on the line he sells. He lacks conviction. Frankly, he thinks it's offensive to try to close someone. He just wastes his time—and your money—in tell-type situations. "I don't want to pressure anyone," he tells himself while hoping against hope someone will rescue him and buy something. In 25 years I've never seen one of this type succeed. The tell-type salesman just doesn't like selling.

Some salesmen just love to hear themselves talk, so all they do is literally teach the prospect all about the product or service. The teach-type salesman merely wishes to demonstrate to the prospect "everything he knows," and he seldom sells. The teach-type salesman doesn't make more closes until he wakes up to the fact that his teaching just isn't a close. He probably comes to the same conclusion the sell-type came to long ago: "Don't fall into the trap of telling and showing the prospect too much. Just sell him."

The sell-type recognizes, first and foremost, that it's better to sell the prospect right away. You completely wrap up the sale; then and only then—after the sale has been made—do you start the teaching process. You hold back on the teaching, but you promise it as part of the deal. "When you own this machine, we will show you how to use it." Make it clear to your prospect that after he owns your product you will provide the know-how he'll need.

The sell-type salesman is ruthlessly sharp in his concentration on the selling position. He is the King of the Closers year in and year out. Questions like "How do you handle this, or that?" he meets with half-answers. He doesn't let it all out at once. The sell-type stays in control. He disciplines himself to the point of not "telling it all" until he has a sale. As a salesperson you need some mystery attached to an item. But the mystery is for your prospects. You know they're going to buy. So you get that over first. You sell them! Any dummy can teach them!

The basic problem of the teach-and-sell salesman is that he forgets why he's selling. He feels that he'll win the prospect by his helpfulness. But this very helpfulness rapidly satiates the prospect, who then turns the salesman off. He feels the salesman is weak. Top salesmen intimidate prospects into buying. The sell-salesman just isn't the nice-guy type. He's tougher, more in control. He's somewhat blunt, uses short sentences, gives the prospect short answers, and rarely goes for the big explanation. The sell-type is cool, not too friendly, refers to people as Mr. Bochwitz, Mrs. Jones, and so on. He's definitely the reserved type until he gets the order. He never

dillies or dallies for a cup of coffee or passes the time of day.
His business is to pass other salesmen—the ones who tell or
teach.

Joe Cannedy of Roberts and Aquire in California told me
of two brothers who bought from him and decided to
celebrate by having lunch with Joe. Each brother had given
him a check for $1,000 as deposit on the purchase. During
lunch the brothers started arguing and asked Mr. Cannedy to
return the checks. They both promptly tore them into small
pieces. Mamma mia! Two $1,000 checks!

So when you do sell, exit smoothly but rapidly. When
you stay after making a sale, you may face a reduced order—
or even a canceled order. Usually the buyer won't go to the
trouble of altering an order if you're not handy. To phone or
write you is too much trouble, so he lets the order ride as
written. Take advantage of your client's laziness. If he weren't
so lazy, he might decide to do the work, make the machine, or
grow the grain himself.

If you are still not convinced that there is a time to talk
and a time not to talk, consider the plight of Ole Johnson, a
shy and fairly committed bachelor.

One evening he was visiting Lena Swenson, an old maid
who lived next door. A poor talker at best, Ole could not think
of much to say. Finally, he blurted out, "Lena, will you marry
me?" To this he got the quickest "Oh yes, Ole" he'd ever
heard in his life.

Again the conversation lagged, and Lena asked, "Ole,
ain't you going to say any more, yah?"

"Aye tank aye said too much already!" sighed Ole.

Don't be a "walking encyclopedia" on your product. Too
much emphasis on facts, figures, nuts and bolts, or extreme
amounts of technical knowledge can overwhelm your prospect. The problem in selling is to avoid giving too much
information about the product. Feed your prospect with an

eyedropper. Don't dump a whole bucket on him. You are better off to have your prospect wanting more of you than a whole lot less of you!

The trick is not to give the prospect too much information. If you overeducate him, he feels secure and doesn't buy. A lot of information just doesn't seem to move merchandise. It satiates the prospect too fast and turns him away from buying. The experienced salesman "saves" information until after the prospect is the owner. You can deliberately hold back information even when you are asked for it. Parry questions, delay, put off answering questions—anything that will keep the customer from getting so full of information he hasn't any room for the desire to buy. It takes a good salesman to sell something. Any gossip can give out information—or misinformation. Delay giving prices as long as possible. Never start a sales presentation by quoting a price. Prospects always want that which they can't have. Get the prospect to "sweat" a little on price.

Many professionals use delaying tactics to hold back information about the product, its use, its price, or its availability. Experiment with it yourself. If a prospect says, "How can your product remove wax?" ask him, "Do you want it if it can handle wax?" I move toward a close by finding out how interested the client is in buying. To do this I give no information, only implied information.

Do you have the alertness, the courage, the audacity, the sharpness to handle your prospects in a delaying fashion? You'll get more closes after you decide to leave the teaching to the teachers. There are more good teachers going into selling than there are good salesmen going into teaching. If you want to make money teaching, talk to the school board about a job. If you want to make money selling, quit teaching and close deals!

A salesman or saleswoman who cannot close is a "conversationalist." If you cannot close, you cannot possibly sell yourself as a salesman. You must find the prospect and close the deal. You must become a closing specialist. If you want to be a realist about selling, you must understand that really the only important thing is to close. So you work to become a strong closer.

The top ingredients in becoming a strong closer are your willingness to try to close right from the start and your persistence in trying to close.

What does it take to close? To start with, it takes charm and good voice modulation. Being agreeable certainly helps. Testimonials, table pounding, persistence, and many other ingredients go into the recipe for closing. In closing, tell your prospect what you believe he wants to hear—that your product can do wonders for him. Don't misrepresent your company, but don't overtalk. Many salesmen talk themselves out of a sale when the sale has already been made! When a sale has been made, shut your order book, shut your mouth, and shut the door as you quickly get out of there!

A third party—another company, another individual— may help you close. Someone who has been in similar circumstances to your prospect's can be a big help. Sometimes customers will believe the third party more than they'll believe you. So who cares? Make the sale with the testimonial of a third party, and laugh your way to the bank!

Get some action in every call. Look for action. Ask for action. Start action. This way you'll move people. Merely to sit there and talk, talk, talk and hope your prospect will "give up" is certainly not salesmanship. Ask him to hold the product, to use the product. Ask him anything to get action, but ask him quick. If you want to give him a lot of words, buy him a book for Christmas.

Close by using proof: guarantees, warranties, statistics, testimonials, third parties, official recognition, performance, facts and figures.

Edward Jorden said, "If you want to sell anything, you must be able to speak the English language. You must be able to speak it so you can be heard in an ordinary room. You must be able to tell what you think about your product and tell it to all the people you possibly can. That is all there is to salesmanship! Except for one thing, I would have added: knowing when to talk and when to shut up.

Little things can cost you a million-dollar order: an outlandish suit, an off-beat tie, an off-color joke, smoking a cigarette. Ninety-nine percent of us want to do business with professionals. The pro sticks to business. He keeps his feelings on politics, sex, religion, and race to himself. Knowing that nobody really cares what his opinions are, he keeps his big mouth shut. The professional is there to sell, not to give away opinions. The pro can sell even if he doesn't have any opinions. The opinionated man can't sell. He gives away his real product: hot air.

People like other people for hundreds of reasons. Friend-liness, cheerfulness, and helpfulness are great, but the quality that leads the field is intelligence—at least as far as salesmen are concerned. As a prospect I ask, "Is he smart enough to help me get what I need?" The salesman who uses his brains will have or develop the other qualities that will put him across: reliability, honesty, frankness, good humor, and many others. One authority stated, "When a salesman sells, he can make more than a brain surgeon . . . when he works." Work to make yourself friendlier. Being pleasant and cheerful sells because it puts the prospect in a better mood. If you don't like to sell to a grouch, cheer him up with your personality!

Do you greet the prospect's secretary, clerks, other employees? Do you deliberately try to sell yourself in a low-keyed, steady way not only to the buyer, but to everyone—especially the buyer's customers? Ask yourself right now: "Do I make a point of being cheerful and pleasant to everyone connected with my prospect? Do I deliberately help him save or make money by my suggestions? Can my intelligence come alive and actually help keep my customer in business? Can I show my customer year in and year out that as a salesman I can literally "make sales" for him time and again? If you do demonstrate this ability, seldom will you be denied an order.

Jim Larson, chairman of the board of Future Homes, New York Mills, Minnesota, a company with 25 salespeople, often tells people that "every time Don Sheehan puts on a seminar for my people, I can actually sit there and see sales climb the week following the meeting." Jim literally becomes a member of my team, as valuable to me as a trusted employee; and, incidentally, Jim got a lot of mileage out of me. This is what is known as scratching each other's back— and we both need the scratching. We both have the itch for the buck!

If you use sales literature, use it very, very sparingly. In fact, I quit using it seven years ago. Brochures are requested by prospects, so have one ready to show, but don't let them keep it. If a customer has the brochure, he feels satisfied by it. He feels he "knows it all" and consequently very often doesn't buy. I believe the only man who wins, when it comes to literature, is the printer. He gets paid for his efforts.

Use a brochure in mail-outs for requested information, but in a face-to-face situation, keep the brochure in a glacine cover. Nine out of ten times a request for a brochure is nothing more than a stall. The customer is just being a "nice guy" to you.

You must remember you don't want him to fatten your ego. You want him to fatten your pocketbook.

7

Separate the Sheep from the Goats

Frank Tusler, 81 years young, and taking one of my classes, used to ask, "Do you want a good year or a great year?" The answer is, of course, that you want a great year. To do this you cannot lose your customer by failing to help him.

Service to a major customer is one of the most difficult tasks in selling. Through absolutely no fault of yours, 20 percent of your customers turn over annually. This means you are already on the way to the graveyard if you "live and die" with one customer. One lost account will then knock you out of business. Don't get yourself in that position. Remember, a centipede can lose quite a few legs and still keep on walking. Your customer will stay with you if you can get him set up to close. Talk to him about profit improvement. Show him how to do it with your services and products. Always have a major plan and a minor plan to get the job done. Be ahead of your customer in showing him how to save more with your product.

With any customer you are always on trial. Just one error

could terminate your business relationship. So you must build confidence with your client by your constant attention to details. The old acid test, the reorder, will be passed only if you keep your customer happy. By skipping a small detail you could lose a big deal. If you expect your customer to stay with you for a year, you have to spend some minutes on the details.

Approximately 80 percent of your business comes from 20 percent of your customers. A big electronics manufacturer proved this to me by analyzing 2,000 customers. Sure enough, 21 percent of the company's customers brought it 79 percent of its total annual volume.

The knack of staying in business is getting and holding certain key customers. Have you taken the time to develop sales strategy to hold and get business? That is, do you systematically offer selling help to customers, lunch with them, assist in their sales efforts? Are you a real help to your customers or are you just a talker?

Perhaps the best way to hold that key business is to keep in mind the difference between a customer and a client: you sell customers, you service clients.

Before qualification takes place, the amateur salesman spends a lot of time in pleasant conversation or preliminary pleasantries. He'll talk weather, or what happened the day or night before in a ball game. A top professional says right away, "Will this purchase be cash or terms?" If the purchase is for cash, he'll follow his normal procedure. If the purchase is for terms, as in the mobile home industry, where 82 percent of all sales are terms, he'll say, "Fine, tell me, have you ever had any judgments, liens, bankruptcies, garnishments that you are ashamed of and would like to tell me about right now?"

Good, straightforward requests for credit information by salesmen are, in most cases, expected by the prospect. In no case should any merchandise be shown before the qualification. During the recession of the mid-seventies, as many as 50 percent of the people applying for home loans nationally were turned down. Many salesmen tell me, "I lost 70 to 80 percent of my customers on credit last month." This tells me they are just not qualifying people enough. If the customer balks at giving credit information, the salesman should level with the prospect and tell him of the high turndown on financing. A salesman from Fargo, North Dakota, tells prospects, "If I'm going to spend half a day of my life to try and get you financing, I need to get all the information I can."

Incidentally, only one man in a company should work with financing, whether he deals with a bank, a savings and loan institution, or a finance company. This way the lender knows to whom he's talking. I find that in "very close ones," the lender will favor a man with whom he's worked.

If the prospect has been through a bankruptcy, it doesn't mean he's impossible. A number of people have told me they were able to get credit for people who had "strung themselves out." If a person has had credit problems, many old pros start with the lender or company credit manager by saying, "This man—or company—has had problems in the past on credit." This clears the air. A good percentage of such people do get additional credit in spite of their bad credit past.

To close a sale and lose it due to poor credit is hard to take. Such disappointments can be avoided in a half-dozen or more ways: fast qualifications, a big down payment, payment in full to establish credit, a 60-day probation period, C.O.D., or lay-by. Don't give up if at first you lose a sale on credit.

One summer, I saw a dealer from Madison, Wisconsin, take one of his prospects to seven different lenders to get him financed. This has to be some kind of world record. The dealer, who did get the financing, told me, "I was very well paid for my extra effort."

Proper qualifications will save you hundreds of hours

spent annually in chasing the "impossibles." In stressful times
of high inflation and limited amounts of credit available, be
prepared to spend as much time selling the lender as you do
selling the prospect. Tell the prospect of this nationwide
credit scarcity. He knows and fears it also. A well-informed
prospect is, frankly, easier to "work." He'll come up with a
higher down payment to help influence his chance with a
lender, salesman, dealer, or company credit department. A
good prospect understands the lender's problems. In good as
well as bad times, prompt payment maintains good relations
with the lender. In the final analysis, lenders determine who
will stay in business. Some business people take their lender
on vacation with them. Take your lender to trade shows, send
industry information to him, keep him on your team. Your
12-months-out-of-the-year campaign to keep your lender
happy should include lunches, visits, good testimonial letters
from satisfied customers, statements—anything your imagination can devise. A well-informed lender will be impressed by
your ability to communicate. This, of course, means you
always tell your banker the truth. Phonies do not communicate; they confuse.

Without proper financing you cannot get the amount of
completed sales you need. If you are unable to get the right
response from one lender, there's nothing wrong in shopping
for another one. Good lenders can be found. Good financial
people know they need you almost as much as you need them.
Lenders make nothing off people who pay cash.

"Bird dogs"—your scouters, qualifiers, part-time people—"warm up" and qualify customers for you. You step in
and close the deals. One year my top "bird dog" made me
many thousands of dollars in extra commissions. You can pay
off yours with dinners, gifts, books, awards, or outright cash
or commissions.

Who can be bird dogs for you? The list is endless: fellow

salesmen, friends, neighbors, local and national associations. Instead of trying to do everything yourself, get your "bird dogs" to help you. Then make it worth their while.

One man helped me sell to more than 800 students. As a "bird dog" he was a "pointer," not a "setter"!

If you sincerely want to close more sales, you must size up people and figure out how best to sell them. Use the descriptions below to plan your attack.

SHEEHAN'S CATALOG OF PROSPECTS

1. *The positive prospect*. Sell him by questions and compliments. He'll usually buy your best item, but be careful! He very likely knows what he is doing, so be on your toes.
2. *The shy, timid bird*. Slow down to five miles per hour with him. He usually buys middle-range items. Be prepared not to talk at all with him.
3. *The detail man*. Listen to him. Then sell him. He's normally a big bore, so he needs a listener.
4. *The snob*. He looks down his nose at salesmen. Don't get excited! A pigeon has to look down his nose at a fox! The fox eats the pigeon; you sell the snob.
5. *The friendly guy*. He rarely buys. Keep him serious. Keep him on the subject. Sell him or you can't afford him as a buddy.
6. *The procrastinator*. Don't ask him to buy. Tell him! He has a hard time making up his mind about anything, so you have to make up his mind for him.
7. *The know-it-all*. Appear to let him run the show, but don't let him run you. Surrender to him, but sell him.
8. *The silent type*. Play his game. Don't talk. Silently write up an order. Then hand it to him to sign.

9. *The cherry picker*. He wants your best, so see that your prices are high enough.

If you know, or have discovered, any other types of buyers, please let me know. I'll help you figure out how to handle them.

8
Record Keeping

Records are a salesman's films of himself in action. He needs records of the number of his sales talks and his attempts to close. He notes whether it was a first, second, or third interview. Without these records, the salesman is operating by the seat of his pants. Football and baseball players all spend hour after hour studying films of themselves to find out what needs watching. It's the same with salesmen, only their films are their sales reports. I've never met a big, consistent producer who isn't a nut on record keeping. The salesman who doesn't keep records doesn't hang up any records either.

Four times I became the worldwide number-one producing salesman selling Dale Carnegie Sales Courses for Mrs. Dorothy Carnegie, successor to her famous husband, simply because I recognized that if I was to become a top producer, I had to excel at record keeping. I needed to devise daily methods of recording my efforts. Sum up your total selling efforts as often as possible so you can find out what you are doing right and what you are doing wrong. Then make the needed adjustments.

...ly method each month was to see 25 managers who were high-level decision makers, 25 small customers who had limited resources but needed the training, and 10 groups where I got multiple orders—a mixed bag of 60 excellent exposures.

I used the same method at St. Cloud, Minnesota, where I quadrupled sales for Colgate Palmolive. I simply sat down and figured out how many customers I had to see daily and what my average order had to be. I actually put down on paper the order I wanted to sell the merchant, and I noted behind each brand (in red pencil) if there was a special deal or discount. By determining a quota of buyers to see daily and by planning orders, I earned the "Outstanding Salesman of the Year" award for the Minneapolis sales area.

Percy Whitley, author of *The Five Great Rules of Selling*, called me the greatest salesman he had seen in his 50 years in business. I appreciated this most generous statement, especially since Percy was rather sparing in his compliments. My 25-25-10 formula won the compliment.

What really was my secret? Well, simply this: to close enough sales I had to see enough people. I had to have the right attitude; I had to present a good sales talk and generate even more closing power.

My record keeping helped me plan, and it can do it for you! Take a minute—or a day—to figure out your best mix of calls or sales talks to the people you serve. For me it is seeing the big guy who can give me a multiple order; calling on the little guy (bear in mind that in the United States, approximately 70 percent of all businesses are owned by sole proprietors) who can give me just one order; and, finally, working on the group, where I can quickly pick up more single orders.

While working for the Carnegie organization, I kept day-by-day records to determine over an 80-month period how many presentations I needed to hit a "maximum month." Fifteen years later I still use the system—trimmed a bit, though, because I'm booked almost 98 percent of the time.

What are your magic figures? What type of people or combination must you see to get better results? Figuring out the answer will give you the key to retailing big-ticket items— paneling, appliances, kitchens, or the mix that gets the desired volume for a given month. What total mix do you need? Can you see where you can put out the effort to get the right mix?

The people who continue to fail in selling can never give me a straight answer to these four questions:

1. How many people do you have to talk to to get a close? What is your closing average?
2. What kind of daily reports do you use to record calls, closes, volume, money collected?
3. What is your goal this month for total volume?
4. Do you have a daily plan laid out for yourself? It should include calls you are going to make, what you are going to say, where to go, what to show—even before you start the day.

What are your answers to these four questions? If you don't have them, you are way behind in your homework.

If you have the answers, you have my permission to put this book down and get out to make the closings—but be back in ten hours! You'll have all the orders you can write up in one evening.

9

Be Ready for Roadblocks

There are plenty of roadblocks ahead. If you do not get ready for them, you are just "winging it"! The negatives are out there blocking your closes. The time to eliminate those negatives is now!

Be alert to the type of buyer who asks question after question but doesn't buy. The professional knows the "Question Box" is on a fishing trip. He's just out to get, by hook or crook, all the information he possibly can. He uses you as an information center. He's shopping you—and anyone else who is unschooled enough to feed this monstrous inquirer.

Play him cool. He'll tip off his behavior pattern by brushing you off when you attempt to close. But you can use this interview as a stepping stone. Deliberately give half answers and ask for more time by suggesting a second and third interview. Tell him this is his "most important purchase." Play his game. For every question he asks about your product or service, politely counter with questions as to what he plans to do if the two of you get together on an order. Be relaxed. Your chances of closing on a "fact-finding interview" are extremely slight . . . so take advantage of it by adopting his own tactics—the ones he's using on you!

In no case should you feel offended by his approach or frustrated by his polite turn-downs to your advances to close. The buyer is doing a job that he's being well paid to do: to find out "everything" about your product or service. This doesn't mean you should exclude salesmanship. Be coy, play on the mysterious, beg for more time to "explain" in full at the next interview.

Just talking to the Question Box can be extremely expensive. A friend of mine, the head of the most successful division of a very large concern, found this out without even trying. My friend and his boss, during a friendly visit with a competitor, were asked "How is that new package going over?" To this innocent question my friend's boss gave a garrulous and very complete account of the success of "that new package." Result: in just a few months the competition was using the same type of successful packaging!

Apart from unexpected dividends, the buyer's obvious strategy is to trim four or five vendors down to two and then pick. Whether you're going to be a primary vendor or a secondary vendor will depend on three things: (1) your behavior toward the buyer, (2) your plan for dealing with the buyer, and (3) your patience.

When your prospect asks question after question before showing any intention to buy, you close in only two interviews out of 100. The average salesman is offended by this. He feels hurt. He doesn't decide quickly enough to be pleasant, helpful, and cheerful. Rather than be annoyed, you should show pleasant surprise and thank him for his interest. Compliment him on his thorough questioning of you. Give him the idea that you are controlling your excitement and that you are not really on guard. Take notes, go slow, work hand in hand with him. Don't act as if he's your adversary; act as though you believe you have a friendship going—but, for heaven's sake, don't brief him on your company's packaging!

Top salesmanship and friendship mean the same to me. I hope it does to you also, because you'll blow this fact-finding interview if you get upset, are not alert, lose your temper, or give curt answers. You'll get greater results by getting in step with the Question Box and by playing his game. When you detect that the whole affair is a "fishing trip" on his part, get all the information you possibly can. Then tell him his business is so important that you'd like to go back to your senior person to get his thinking on the plan, that you need the help and benefit of the senior's expertise, that you'd like to come back and present a well thought-out plan to your client. Maybe he will get garrulous and give you one of his company secrets!

Risky? Not really. Your chances of closing in this type of situation are so slim anyway that your second interview step allows you to control the situation. Most of your competitors will tell it all in the first interview, so don't you do that. Do not give out exact prices—or exact anything—in that first interview. You do not want the type of comparison where they concentrate on costs only: "Mine is $4.25 per ounce, the competitor's is $5.09." You lessen your chances of closing if the first interview degenerates into a price-bargaining session. If you allow this, you literally have no cause for a second interview. You have told your story, and you are at the mercy of the "committee"—the group that now has to make a decision with only part of the needed information about your proposition.

The right way is to hold off on the complete story until you have a chance to reorganize and regroup your forces. Then you start building your plan, piece by piece, with the help of others from your office. It's then that you go on to a

Total Plan that stresses the benefits of your services—your backup people, your facilities, your history. It amounts to the Total Offer Concept (TOC) that we discuss in Chapter 10.

The average salesman is caught off guard by a flood of questions. Your best approach is to welcome the buyer's inquiry; live through it gracefully, but stall on prices, delivery, and so on. Seek the second interview with an "expert"—if necessary—from the home office. Your best plan is to simply ask:

"When do you need all this information?"
"How can we best help you? What do you expect if we are selected as your vendor?"
"What other vendor are you working with on this?"
"Would you need any special considerations, like terms, delivery, quantities, sizes, shapes?"

Be all business about this. You're dealing with a buyer who definitely is out to get "information." He may not intend to buy 25¢ worth, but you can't overlook what he might purchase. Size him up. Study his situation. Could he buy $500,000 worth? $100,000 worth? In one year or five years? What are his potential customer profit and commission worth to you and the company? Yes, use your pencil. Ask questions. Is it possible he could be a Goliath? Or just a nice profitable middle-ground customer? Or is he a loser?

Your behavior is being watched. The potential buyer knows he'll have to deal with you. Are you easy to buy from, or are you abrasive? Do you wear well? This is part of what's going on in the buyer's mind.

One authority estimated that 87 percent of all sales and jobs are lost and marriages fail—because people rub others the wrong way. Be on guard! Watch the little courtesies; control your human relations. Then it's possible to close the sale in the next interview.

The plan should have two options for the prospective prospect. Always give him something, when and if he chooses you. When you offer a "take it or leave it" plan, more often than not the buyer picks the "leave it" option.

In selling my courses on a national basis, I use the "short term" (three-month) course. This keeps prospects concentrating on the short or long term, not just on "anything or nothing." Do the same. Present your clients with a choice so that either way you win!

To strengthen your plan, it always helps to bring in an expert, if the situation warrants it. Ask for a week, if possible, to come back. Have plenty of evidence that you have buyer satisfaction: written testimonials, photographs, charts, and the like. Bring up the fact that you have warehouse closeouts, special programs for promotions coming up, discontinued merchandise—anything that may legally warm up your prospect to accepting your total program of purchase.

In summary, when your prospect asks question after question but doesn't buy:

- Recognize he's on a fact-finding or fishing trip. Watch your behavior. Don't be annoyed.
- Play his game. Politely get all the information you can.
- Be careful not to quote any specifics, such as prices, delivery, and so on. Stall for time.
- Ask for a second interview to develop a plan with your experts, then give him your Total Offer Concept (see next chapter).

Smile to yourself, inside, when you recognize the situation. Then control it with a "planned" interview. Then you are a top strategist, a member of the elite, the 2 percent who really care about selling bigger orders all year round!

10
If You Want to Fly, Too High Is Better Than Too Low

"Not to laugh, not to lament, not to curse, but to understand."

—Spinoza

"And to close."

—Don Sheehan

How do you handle the regular or prospective buyer who says, "Your prices are too high; you're higher than your competition"?

The green salesman hates the expression, "Your prices are too high," and the professional salesman works hard not to get into that situation. The old pro has learned to present his offer correctly so he gets the price complaint less often.

Your prospect could be using this as a ploy, or he may be in dead earnest. Always watch him carefully to detect if he is truly sincere or merely testing his chances of getting an even lower price from you. In either case statements such as the following could well turn the situation in your favor: "Mr.

Prospect, there is an old economic law in America that never changes. You usually get what you pay for. Do you believe that, Mr. Prospective Buyer?" Or if he's a regular buyer whom you know, merely say, "We need to get those prices, because we really want to stay in business this year and next year so we can serve you better." You can also cite an example: "One of America's largest retail firms, Sears and Roebuck, actually works closely with manufacturers to see that profit margins are maintained! My firm could be of no value to your firm and your planning if we become a casualty in the long run and go out of business. And we could go out of business if we don't manage our prices right." I learned this from a Schaak Electronics salesman. He said, "We want to stay in business too bad to give merchandise away for the sake of making sales." You might also tell him, "You only cry once when you buy quality!"

The professional salesman doesn't get himself into price jams. He thoroughly schools himself on why he has to get the right price. Mr. Heinz Goldman of Zurich, Switzerland, calls this the "Total Offer Concept." This means he tells the prospective buyer the history of his firm—number of years in the business, the management quality of his company, what services the buyer receives when he purchases, the city desk, quick delivery, the reliable people serving the customer, the credit department's reasonable terms. This Total Offer Concept tells the buyer that your company will be in business for a long, long time; that it's no "basement operation" with a high probability of failure; that it can abundantly supply the buyer in good times and bad.

So the professional, before he gives a price, reminds the buyer gently and pleasantly of his Total Offer Concept and quotes the prices softly. Never shout your price. Be a "wooer"—you get a much better reception! You may prefer to write prices on a small piece of paper and in small script. This is a subtle suggestion that the price is really very small.

The history of American price-cutting firms has not been good. With rare exceptions they have gone out of business. So stick to your guns. Stay firm on your prices. Be proud of your prices. Plan on getting your prices. If you use the right strategy, you will get them. Do not show hostility when challenged on price.

Dress well—white shirt, shined shoes. Give them the IBM Salesman Look. IBM salesmen (and I've trained dozens of them) are the best-dressed salesmen in the world. They can't budge a nickel on their prices either.

Being sincere helps you overcome price objections. I've seen hundreds of winning performances by well-dressed salesmen who were pleasant and sincere and who understood the Total Offer Concept. Buyers used the old "your prices are too high" bit, but these level-headed salesmen convinced their clients that the prices were just right. (Some things have to be just so high. Just ask any truck driver who tried to squeeze under too low a bridge.)

You must be prepared to tell your complete story as well as possible before giving prices. My research tells me that only about 10 percent of American buyers are price buyers. The remaining 90 percent can be persuaded to pay your prices.

FIVE WAYS TO GET YOUR PRICE

1. Dress very well.
2. Be pleasant.
3. Be sincere.
4. Use the Total Offer Concept before giving your price.
5. Keep your cool. The buyer may be stalling.

Understand that whatever you charge, you'll always get resistance. It's natural for buyers to resist. Don't take it personally! The statement "I want to shop around" is usually not valid. I have found that more than 50 percent do not shop

around, because they're too lazy or because they're busy
people who do not have time to shop around. It's absolutely
normal for buyers to hesitate. Don't abandon your prices
because of this hesitation. Remember the truck driver! You
too can crack your head on a "low bridge."

In a recent case, my prospective buyer said, "In looking
at your plan and Dale Carnegie's, I haven't decided which I'm
going to take. You're higher than they are." I immediately
punched the TOC button (Total Offer Concept) and said, "I
try to personalize my plan even more by giving no-charge
refresher sessions six months and one year later. At these
sessions I provide individual help."

This extra effort meant that the student wrote out a check
for nearly $400 to my firm—rather than to a competitor.
Why? Because I offered him an immediate low-cost service.
You can do the same. Be prepared to do a little extra to move a
long way. Agree to extras that cost you little or nothing, such
as delivering the merchandise (if it's small) in your car during
your lunch hour. Your hustle will usually win the battle of
price and get you the order.

Use good, colored visual aids of the product itself in an
attractive way. By doing this you'll usually lessen price
resistance. Hold off giving the price until the very end! If you
begin with price, you become a quoter—you're practicing
pricemanship or, worse yet, give-awaymanship, but not
salesmanship. Stop and think this out for a minute. If you're
getting a lot of resistance on price, chances are 99 to one that
your presentation is weak, that you're not giving a complete
presentation, or that you have put very little or no effort into
building up the Total Offer Concept part of your offer. Ask
yourself these questions:

1. Is it possible my sales talk is weak or incomplete?
2. Have I degenerated into a quoter, a price bargainer? Am I
   giving the stuff away?

3. How determined am I to get my prices?
4. Am I honestly proud of my prices?
5. Am I starting with prices, or do I delay giving prices? The longer you delay giving prices, the better.

Do not let the price objection get to you. Someone will always be lower than you. You'll invariably lose some orders because of price, but ask yourself if you really lose! Sometimes you're better off not getting the business. In Minneapolis, we have a $140 million Investors Diversified Service building. It's the tallest building west of Chicago, a real wonder of glass and glitter. I congratulated one big operator who got a big contract to perform work in the building. He grimaced and said, "I really didn't win. Our prices were too low to earn decent profits."

Go over this material. Bone up on the facts you need. Try just one idea for a full week—dressing better, using the TOC, or holding back on price. When you see what one idea will do, you will be eager to use the whole bag of tricks.

Finally, so that price isn't thrown at you continuously, do a top job of selling yourself to the buyer whenever possible. Nothing beats basic courtesy: listening attentively, opening doors, and standing when women enter a room. Small, inexpensive gifts—books, calendars, unusual writing pens— can move price discussion into the background. Being cheerful often sells you to the buyer without his fully realizing it. You spent enough in dressing to look sharp, so don't skimp on something like cheerfulness. It costs you nothing.

Don't underestimate the total power of being the personality type who just plain pleases prospects and customers. People buy from people they like—regardless of price! Furthermore, smart buyers know that to get a "price deal" they must give up something—in delivery, service, quality, or payment terms.

Sell the buyer, driving home the fact that you intend to

stay in business next year. He may have price problems too. You'll not only get more orders but be laying the ground work for a long-lasting right-price relationship. Remember, America's business history has not treated the price-cutter too well. Just check the tens of thousands of annual business failures. My experience tells me that in the last two recession years, approximately 50 percent of the businesses that closed their doors forever folded basically because they didn't maintain their prices. They lost because they were not sold on what to charge for their goods or services.

Think of your price as your throat. Don't cut it!

Memorize this formula when your buyer sings that worn-out ditty, "Your price is too high":

P—Pleasing dress.

R—Remember to sell and forget price.

I—In business is where you want to stay.

C—Courtesy.

E—Explain the Total Offer Concept.

If you prefer to think of "price" as your "throat," how about this memory device?

T—Total Offer Concept.

H—Hide the price, not your smile.

R—Remain in business by charging enough.

O—Overcome competition; don't meet it!

A—Anticipate price resistance!

T—Tune up your sales talk!

Another aspect of adapting to "Your price is too high" or "Your price is high" is to close at once! Many sales authorities do not recognize that criticism of your price can be the strongest buying signal the buyer can flash at you.

I truly believe that out-and-out criticism of price should be directly challenged by the salesman by an actual closing attempt. As an example, one of my prospective buyers objected to my charging him $1,000 to teach seven salesmen for one full day. He simply stated, "That's too much money!" Without pausing I said, "I can be in Seattle, October 2, to train your people at the Hyatt House." Without hesitating he said, "I'll take it." If I had told him the additional benefits of the training, I might well have lost the sale.

Next time you get buyer resistance, go for the close instead of giving additional explanation. Remember, these are trying times. Respect a buyer's objection to price and price increases, but don't give up your position. If you stand firm on your price offer, you'll be in business next season—and your firm could be around to capitalize on the Tricentennial! Make a direct appeal to your prospect's sense of honor. If he sells goods or services, ask him point blank how his company salesmen are trained. Ask him if he doesn't think a good company history of proven, consistent quality, delivery, terms, plus the determination to stay in business, are worth more than a basement or a one-shot operation. Tell him you believe in his company and that you hope he'll believe in your company.

Too strong? Not on your life! Tell it like it is. Show it like it is. Then ask him to buy. Don't feel bad in the least about spending 20 minutes to an hour in handling the price.

Remember this difference between the novice and the pro. The green salesman cuts his price—and his own throat; the pro cuts away the objections to price. When giving the price, state it, but do not pause. Continue talking after you give the price by saying, "The investment is $1,000, and for that you get first-of-the-week delivery, thirty-day billing, plus guaranteed merchandise." Say it softly and look the prospect in the eye!

11
The Buck Passer

The buck passer who tells you he must talk to his partner, his wife, his lawyer, or his board of directors must not be allowed to handle you! Careful research on this tactic of prospective buyers has convinced me that this is a predetermined way of putting off making any decision! It's prearranged with his partner or his board. The prospective buyer feels very safe with this ploy. It sounds so good to the seller than he seldom, if ever, challenges the buyer. It's like a Supreme Court decision. No one wants to disturb this type of buyer; no one dares to question him about his intentions.

I'm convinced that in 50 percent of the cases, the prospective buyer is a buck passer, nothing more than a glorified procrastinator! One of the best ways to handle this seemingly impossible situation is to use the "just suppose" technique. When the person states he must confer with this one or that one, quickly corner him by stating, "Just suppose your partner (or your board) says, 'Yes, let's do it.' Now if this third party agrees that this idea or plan is a good one, then will you agree to the plan or idea?" Usually it takes prospective buyers by surprise; and, normally, up to 75 percent of them will go for the idea.

Your next step is to continue the challenge by asking for the third party's phone number and by having the prospective buyer dial the third party right on the spot! He introduces you, then you take the receiver and proceed to set up an appointment with the third party—lawyer, partner, board, or a bank president. When you meet this third party, begin your conversation in this manner: "Mr. First Party has already agreed he likes my idea and would like me to get your thinking." You must take charge in a positive way, assert yourself with an air of confidence. You will then be prodding the procrastinator.

Closing ratios are pitifully small when the buyer takes your presentation and attempts to repeat it to a third party. You might as well forget it!

His wife, lawyer, or partner will, as a rule, talk him out of trying something new or different—or, in fact, of trying anything. So challenge the buck passer right off the bat. Clear the air by asking: "If the third party likes it, do you want it?" It is logical, and it works smoothly if you have the gumption to try it. You will try it if you are sick and tired of hearing, "I have to talk to the third party."

If the prospective buyer requests that he convey the message to the third party, discourage his action at once! Tell him your experience tells you that, without exception, the third party brings up questions only you can answer. Be firm! Mr. First Party—the one who says, "I want to talk to my partner, my wife"—will rarely earn a close for you. You will never get a sale anytime a first party converses with a third party. It just doesn't happen! Don't let it happen to you. If you can't talk to the decision maker, pleasantly withdraw from the situation.

Several years ago I helped get a 97 percent sales increase for the Future Homes Company of Wadena, Minnesota. It amounted to an all-time record. Twenty-five salespeople sold almost 100 percent more in a four-month period! So I approached the manager, James Jager, about additional manager training. It was a $5,000 package, and all the managers would be exposed to the training. He told me, "I'll have to talk to the managers and see if they want the training. You know, we just finished your sales training."

I said, "Jim, let's suppose you talk to them and they agree that the management thing would be a good idea, would you then honor my invoice for $5,000?"

He said, without hesitation, "Absolutely." I then proceeded to handle the situation in this manner. "Jim, let's get all those managers together—all eight of them—and sit them down and tell them the good news of manager seminars." We set a date, and I'm happy to say they took the manager course.

Handled in any other way—allowing Jim to handle the presentation—would have produced a different kind of result. I've found that when Mr. First Party does your selling for you, he invariably reports: "They thought it was great . . . for next year!," "Wrong time of year," or "Too expensive." You lose, Mr. First Party loses, the third party loses. Everybody loses simply because you didn't use the "just suppose" technique. If Mr. First Party persists in delivering your message for you, you indeed have a very serious situation. Back off from him; relax; change the subject—you could be severely battering his ego. Then come back to the issue: "Who will deliver your presentation to Mr. Third Party?" (Offense is always better than defense.) Tell Mr. First Party sweetly, "Let me handle this presentation. I'm sure you wouldn't want someone else handling your presentation. I'd be more than glad to do it and want you there to hear every word I say to your people." This usually stops buyers cold! They can usually see your point at once. The honest procrastinator knows that if he had to deliver a message on his product, he would want to do it himself—in his own way, using his own method and with his own words—so he should respect your request to deliver your own sales talk. As a buck passer, he can easily see the "value" of letting you do your own work.

All this must be done with dispatch. The longer the delay, the less chance of closing. So on the phone, set up an appointment right on the spot. If the partner is out, set up an appointment for that afternoon or the next day and tell Mr. First Party you would like to have him in on it.

Why does Mr. First Party use the buck-passing tactic? He is insecure—he doesn't want to make an error. But don't delay! Attempting to cure procrastination with hesitation is like trying to cool your soup by blowing on it with a torch! My 25 years of selling tell me that by accepting delays you lose 95 percent of the time. The odds are just not with you. So talk firmly and pleasantly with the procrastinator to convince him of the reasonableness of your cause. Produce, when possible, typewritten testimonials, letters from companies that have enjoyed substantial benefits from your products or services. Then point out that before they accepted your efforts, a similar situation existed between the first and third parties. Gently, but unemotionally, point out that as a second party to the successful transaction, you played the part of go-between. Point out that you can handle all the details and show how many steps and how much time it would save Mr. First Party. What could appeal more to a buck passer? If he were ambitious enough to do the job himself, he wouldn't be passing the buck!

Cardinal Richelieu said we all must practice diplomacy daily. Here's your chance to improve on the famed prelate. You could even be a Henry Kissinger! Here's your chance to use high-level tactics. Rehearse your strategy in advance.

Then challenge the buck passer at once with the "just suppose" technique. This is where you "eliminate the negative and accentuate the positive." The audacity of your move—your self-assured assumption of a positive result—is frankly intriguing to Mr. First Party. Many times, I've seen first-party people perk up. They get a mental picture of third parties smiling at Mr. First Party for being smart enough to go to the real smartie, Mr. Third Party! "Here," says Mr. Procrastinator to himself, "is buck-passing of the best kind! I get the peddler off my back and the boss on my side!"

The strategy to dislodge Mr. First Party as a presentor to the third party is always risky. He can clam up, feel insulted, terminate negotiations right on the spot. I've seen out-and-out rejections on the spot, but when I knuckled under to the buck passer's way of thinking—letting him be the presentor—I nearly always lost. I finally came to my sanity—after one loss after another. Today, it's either my way, or I withdraw with a brief explanation: "Mr. First Party, my experience has taught me that I do my best work when I handle the assignment from start to finish. I wish to withdraw from this situation, simply because right at the start you are unable to allow me to handle the deal." Even if he allows me to withdraw, I still have the satisfaction of standing my ground and holding to my methods of doing business. I can walk away knowing I'm better prepared to handle the next "I want to talk to Mr. Third Party." This way I'm finished with the situation. My mind holds no anticipation for that client. My mind is freed up for the future buyer with whom I really can transact business.

In summary: do these things when confronted with, "I want to talk to my partner, my board, my people, my committee, my foreman":

• Challenge him right off with the "just suppose" technique: "If your partner likes it, Mr. First Party, will you accept the plan or idea?"

- When Mr. First Party wants to do your selling for you to Mr. Third Party, be diplomatic, and tell him you are sure he would not want you to deliver his presentation if he were in your shoes. Be firm. Tell him your experience tells you third parties always have questions that first parties have difficulties answering.
- Even if you lose by using the suggested method, you at least walk away intact; but, count on it, you win time in and time out with this technique. It gives you that certain "mental toughness" that Vince Lombardi made use of to turn out championship teams. It will win for you too!
- If a committee has to decide on your proposition and you're not allowed in, give the presenter a tape cassette to play in front of the committee. It does work! At least you'll know your competitor wasn't smart enough to use it!

12
Writer's Cramp

On a big-ticket item, the prospect is ready to close, but he has writer's cramp—he just won't sign. Now what?

The type of close that I'm going to suggest to solve this common problem is what I call "The Buyer Protection Agreement." It has been used successfully in selling big-ticket items such as big boats, airplanes, cars, and appliances. It was even used in selling jets to the State of Israel!

This is the scenario: the salesman "has sold his head off, spilled his guts all over the floor," used his "Sunday punch"— all to no avail. The prospect nods agreement and seems pleased, and all appears well—but there is absolutely no action from him. He seems hesitant, interested one moment, neutral the next. The sale is in suspended animation. What do you do? Where do you start, what do you say? Most salespeople stand there in a fog of indecision. In their minds the situation is just one step above hopeless. Yet it isn't!

Here's how you step into this zero situation: "Mr. Prospect, have you ever heard of our Buyer Protection Plan?"

Of course he hasn't. You have never told him—but now you
do. "Mr. Prospect, you give me a deposit on this item, and I'll
give you a written agreement to do these three things:

1. If the product goes up in the next 30 days, you'll own it at
   the old price.
2. If the product goes down in the next 30 days, you'll own
   it at the lower price.
3. If you should change your mind in the next 72 hours, for
   any reason, we'll gladly refund your deposit."

Then ask, "Doesn't that sound fair?" Even Diogenes, that
famous Greek with the lantern, never came across a more
honest deal than that!

We're converting "walkout" customers all over America.
Rudy Boschwitz of Plywood, Minnesota stepped into a sales
situation in Chicago, where his president, John Loffler, had
worked on a buyer for 40 minutes without result. Boschwitz
very quickly used the Buyer Protection Close for a sale!

My records for the past two years show that by using this
close many salesmen report up to 90 percent "saves." In other
words, if 100 people accepted the plan, up to 90 percent
completed the purchase. Some point out that this is like
putting people on "lay-by." Yes, it is, and what's so wrong
with that? Salesmen who are using it, like George Philips of
Cheyenne, Wyoming, swear by it. I have salesmen in Seattle,
Las Vegas, San Francisco, and all over the country who use it
as a last resort and profit by it. Yes, it is a last-resort close.
You use it only when the prospective buyer is leaving the
store. Normally you'd regret his leaving; this way you profit
from his leaving.

Tell him, point blank, that if he finds another piece of
merchandise that has all the features, guarantees, warranties
your product has, plus the after-sale service your company
has, he should take the competition's deal; if not, then he

should come back to you. If he does come back for a refund, you still have another opportunity to sell him.

This technique, the "Buyer Protection Plan," is for the customer who tells you, "I want to shop around." As I said, only 50 percent actually shop around. The rest are too lazy— or lack the time to look.

You should always be ready with a clipboard and an agreement so you can write up the order easily and freely without fumbling. You should carry a minimum of three pens with you at all times. Buyers are sometimes like steel: tough. But when they're *hot*, they are like highly heated steel: malleable! So close them! It doesn't matter if you're in an airplane, airport, tunnel, ship at sea, warehouse, top of a tower. Do it now! And don't call the agreement a "contract." It scares the prospect. An agreement is the same thing but doesn't sound as harsh. Do not ask prospects to sign, merely ask them to "okay the agreement." In Madison, Wisconsin, a salesman needed signatures from both husband and wife, so he asked them to okay the agreement. They promptly did so.

Don't give up when you run into a buyer who just won't close. Use the Buyer Protection Plan and see the difference. Soon you'll have six to ten prospects that you never had before.

A salesman from St. Paul, Minnesota, told me the Plan accounts for up to 20 percent of his business every year. No wonder he is always in the top 5 percent of several hundred salesmen selling appliances, furniture, kitchens, and the like.

The Plan also demands a strong follow-up to complete the sale. Enthusiastically follow up on the deal so your sale is completed in the specified time, say 30 days. The Plan itself solves the big problem of walkouts; the other half of the sale, a strong follow-up, winds up things with a close. Use the phone, the mail, a personal visit—all are great. The best approach is to use the phone and cheerfully say, "The merchandise is all ready and shined up. When you come over to pick it up, I'll be ready to help you load it."

In summary, on big-ticket items, when the prospect seems ready to close, use the Buyer Protection Plan as a last resort.

Remember, you're saving sales on this technique. You could increase your annual closing rate from 10 percent to 20 percent or more, but you must be well rehearsed and have your management's acceptance of the plan. One extra close a week means an additional 50 or more closes per year!

Understand that people would prefer saying yes to you. It's harder for them to say no. You can make it even easier for them to say yes. Allow them the courtesy, at least, of the Buyer Protection Plan. Your buyer will surely say something like: "That sounds fair," "I'll take it," "Say that again," or "I'd be crazy not to accept that."

Do you have the fortitude to use these proven techniques in your everyday selling? Will you adapt these techniques to your way of selling? I believe you will! Only by learning from others will you ever reach your potential. The have-beens are the ones who claim—without even trying it—"That won't work on my customers," or "My territory is different." That brand of thinking is loser rationale. Sure there are differences, but there is nothing more consistent than human nature.

As a salesman, you must do many things, some of which are to excite people to action. The Buyer Protection Plan can do that for you. The astute salesman knows he has to increase the buyer's urgency if he's going to get action.

George O'Neil of Roberts and Acquire Company in Novato, California, told me, "There's no reason why a prospect cannot be converted into a customer." If the situation seems to the buyer to lack urgency, it is up to you to add that element. It is the sizzle that sells the steak.

George O'Neil, in my mind, is one of America's premier

big-ticket salesmen. His earnings are close to the $100,000 mark in annual commmissions. He dresses perfectly, thinks brilliantly, and makes almost half as much as the president of the United States. George O'Neil sells mobile homes—400 of them in three years. This has to be some kind of record! George is a technique man. He's 100 percent technique. If a buyer tells him, "I'm just looking," George simply asks, "How long have you been looking?" and uses the reply to start closing!

Experts state that 10 percent of the people selling big-ticket items make $25,000 per year, and only 2 percent of our big-ticket salesmen earn $50,000 a year. My ten years of travel all over America has proven this to be more than true.

Big-ticket salespeople do one of three things: (1) teach their customers all about the product, (2) tell them all about the product, or (3) sell them the product. The secret is not to give too much information until the buyer owns the item. Too often a salesman cannot close the big-ticket sale because he satiated the prospect with too much product knowledge, and the prospect feels he already owns the product, and therefore lacks the motivation actually to purchase. So keep that prospect hungry until you've okayed an agreement or have money down. Deliberately put off choice pieces of information. Say, "When you own this, I sure want to tell you more about this feature," or "When this is operational, I want to spend an hour with you and your people showing you the correct procedure." Resist the temptation to spill all the beans. Put off the urge to teach the buyer everything on the spot. If you tell everything, you may make your prospect happy, but he will be an uncommitted buyer. In fact, if you talk for more than three minutes, you have been too long-winded. Let your prospect share the conversation.

Don't be afraid to tell prospects, point blank, that you'll fill them in on several vital points after they have purchased.

Give only partial replies or you'll flood their minds with inessential facts and figures. That only tends to make people hesitate. Your job is to sell first, then explain in detail later.

On big-ticket items, the temptation is to give out literature to prospective buyers. Don't do it! Have a big book to show them, or show them a brochure but tell them it is the only one you have with you. Handing prospects literature gives them just another excuse to go home and "think it over." Prospects feel safe with the brochure. They feel it's a quick substitute for facts and figures. They read and read, but don't really have to decide. After years of studying the pros and cons of handing literature to prospects, I decided to advise companies selling big-ticket items not to give out literature, because it gets buyers off the hook—they don't have to make a decision. Your advertising agencies will fight this, but my experience tells me it's only a put-off, an exchange of "lumber," a polite way of saying no. The only ones I've seen win by giving out literature have been the advertising agencies and their printers. Instead of spending $5,000 on literature, spend it on training your sales force to close sales! So please, no literature! If worst comes to worst, "lend" your only copy for 24 hours, then set up an appointment and go back to get the brochure—and close. I've not given out printed literature on my business for seven years, yet I've quadrupled my sales. Try it!

13
Tomorrow
Never Comes

"I'll make a decision next week" is a piece of dialog from a performance that should get an academy award, an Oscar. It's hard to top, but remember, it is tough for your prospect to come up with an encore. So come on, Rock Hudson, get on with your act! Check his voice modulation. Is it a firm "I'll make a decision next week," or is it a passive, low-conviction type of statement? If he comes out with a firm "Check with me next week for a decision," you can do something that few salesmen are smart enough to do. Thank him, right on the spot, for being concerned enough about your proposition to use his valuable time to even consider it. This way you're rendering him a type of compliment for his consideration. My experience tells me a softening of his attitude toward you takes place. You're likely to find this well-trained prospect just a little more receptive toward your next strategy.

Remember the old saying: "Tomorrow never comes"? Well, if that is the case, what chance has "next week"? So get moving!

Should you detect a warming up of the prospect due to your "thank you" approach, merely let the conversation die down to five miles per hour and gently take out your appointment book; loosely page to one week from today. Ask in a low-toned voice, "What time would you like to see me a week from today?" Normally he doesn't expect this counter-type strategy, so he fumbles around a bit. Say nothing. Just concentrate on the schedule you have in front of you. If he says nothing, merely say, "Would you prefer me to be here in the morning or in the afternoon?"

The request for a second appointment or for a delayed decision is a fair one. Seldom does a buyer resent it or feel pressured by it. Many welcome the approach, because you are helping the buyer come to a wise decision. You are also diplomatically checking to see if the prospect is really interested or is just putting you off.

If you detect a mechanical, passive tone as he promises, "I'll make a decision next week," you might challenge him with soft-spoken emotional appeals: "Do you really think your situation will change that much in just seven days?" or "Let me write the order now, date it for a week away. I'll hold it until then and confirm the order by phone next week," or "I can save you an extra 1 percent if you place the order today." Sometimes you can trade off something of value: "I'll add an extra 30 days to your warranty if you place the order now."

The professional is always prepared for stalls, put-offs, procrastination, indecision. The professional saves something extra for a right-now decision. He or she knows that any delay in a sale for any reason always cuts the chances of closing. People change their minds; people easily get disenchanted, become ill, die. People get fired. Anything can happen when there are delays. So, to close is the very highest of priorities in selling. If no close seems possible, then strategies, tactics, and scheming are very much in order.

The plain truth of the matter is that the expression "I'll make a decision next week" could mean two dozen things. To name a few of them: "I want you to sweeten my deal a little." "I want you to sweat more for my order." "Your competitor will be here this afternoon. I want to see what she has to say." "I need to get further instructions from my boss before I can move." Or, "How do I get rid of this guy? He doesn't have a chance."

All these things could be flashing through the prospect's mind. It's your job to find out, diplomatically, where you stand with him. You could be wasting his time and yours. It is bad enough wasting his time, but your time, too? Ugh!

If your judgment tells you you're "on the bottom side," don't be afraid to ask him point blank, "How much of a chance do I have?" It's a fair question and usually invokes a straight answer. You at least know where you stand.

You might also say: "It's obvious to me you're resistant to deciding. Do you mind if I ask you why? Have I done anything to cause you to delay your decision?" or "Please tell me what else I can do that might help you come to the right decision."

Do these things work? I'll tell you they do! I feel the bulk of all sales are closed with the fourth and fifth attempts to close.

I remember when Louis Aronson balked at my request to sell him two straight carloads of Ajax Cleanser. He just wouldn't hear of it and said, "I should order a two-year supply just because you've a special offer on it? Nothing doing!" He got up, put on his coat, and was going out the warehouse. I said, "Louis, what would you do if I came back here within 72 hours with signed orders for both carloads?" He looked startled and said, "If you can sell that many cases, you deserve the two cars."

It was 1,000 cases! I was prepared enough to feel I at least had a chance to sell that many. I already had planned my itinerary so I would hit all the towns in his Minnesota county, including Little Falls, Genola, Harding, and Pierce. I "blitzed" Morrison county in the next 72 hours. I brought in orders for 950 cases. He read each one carefully, looked at each signature, and checked the quantity on a nearby machine. His hesitation evaporated: "Where do I sign for the two cars?" I had the order made out in advance, and he quietly gave me his okay. Wow! Wow! What a signature! It was a big circle, like a target. When I left him his copy, he offered me a job selling for him, right on the spot. He introduced me glowingly to his wife, Molly. I told him I was pleased, but I had just been named Salesman of the Year for Colgate Company in a six-state area and had been presented with a trophy by the sales and marketing executives of Minneapolis. I told him I was flattered by his offer, but I just couldn't consider it. What he should have done was ask me: "Well, will you let me show you how you can be Salesman of the Century working for me?"

"Decision next week" tells you a lot. It tells you to challenge the "next-week buyer" with everything you have at your command. It is not a signal to stop and feel sorry for yourself. When you hear "next week," start to dig. Keep negotiations open by offering little extras, little trade-offs. But act! Don't fold your tent too speedily, or the buyer will think less of you. Your lack of conviction helps unconvince him.

Many times the actual physical act of staying with your prospect for 10 to 20 minutes more—just plain standing your ground—can get positive results. Offering additional benefits and more services can save the day, but you must take the time to stay. Don't run! Politely stand your ground. You'll be delighted how many times you'll be rewarded with an order.

Try the "camping technique": the salesman stands his ground, in a gentle and professional way, until he wears his prospect out. In frustration the prospect will just give you the order as he grumbles, "I may just as well get it over with. Where do I sign?" or "Man, you're determined. Wish my people had half your guts. I'll take your deal!" or "I'll give you the order today if you can do this for me. Can you do this?"

The "camping technique" works! Stand fast. Do not abandon your position. Do not surrender!

If you need further proof of the value of tenaciousness, here is a story from the Lord himself! The account is in the first five verses of the eighteenth chapter of St. Luke's Gospel, in case you want to check it.

Anyway, an unjust judge kept putting off a widow who had a serious complaint against an enemy. Finally he gave in: "Maybe I have neither fear of God nor respect for man, but since she keeps pestering me, I must give this widow her just rights or she will persist in coming and worry me to death."

Are you going to let a little old widow outsell you?

In summary, to the statement, "I'll make a decision next week," do these things to help salvage the situation:

- Check the prospect's voice modulation to see if he's firm or passive.
- Thank him for his consideration (a compliment).
- Attempt to set up a second appointment.
- If you get a passive response, ask him if he really thinks his situation will be different next week.
- Be prepared to offer extra services or other advantages to get a signed order today.
- Ask the prospect where you stand with him and what you can do to improve your position.
- Challenge him—as I did with Louis Aronson.
- Use the "camping technique." Just sit it out with him. You might just wear him out a bit.

14
Rocking Chair Blues

"Our present supplier is doing a good enough job" is a statement I've heard at least 100 times in the past 25 years. It's really not too different from "I've a relative in the business" or "My neighbor has been selling to us for years."

Hearing this statement seems like hitting a stone wall. It's like being hit by a ton of bricks. No way is it easy to overcome. It speaks of loyalty, friendship, years of doing business together, parties, association meetings, buyer and seller understanding of each other's methods. The customer even accepts the supplier's idiosyncrasies.

Both are obviously joined in a duet, and their favorite song is "Those Old Rocking Chair Blues."

Ninety-eight percent of all salesmen "walk" when they hear a prospect say "We do business with the Smith Company and have for 42 years." Seldom is this objection answered realistically. This situation is tough. My solution is not a quick cure, but it has worked for me and hundreds of other salesmen. It is worth at least some effort on your part to study the logic of my plan.

When the prospective customer kicks out with "Our present supplier is doing well enough," I act alarmed and counter with: "That position could be very costly to you and your firm. It could leave you extremely vulnerable—wide open to a number of crises. Let me explain in detail why I say that." I then present three very good points:

1. Two hundred years of American business have taught us to have at least two suppliers. Economic and political conditions can quickly change. Wars can break out; populations can shift.
2. The 1980s are already forecast to be times of definite shortages of every type of material from apples to zinc.
3. Annual rates of 12,000 business failures and 25,000 or more mergers dictate an open mind toward a second supplier.

To get your one-supplier customer out of his rocking chair, you do one thing and one thing only. You cast doubt on his idea of relying on a single supplier. Your interview is set up for the long run—to get him stirred up and to condition his mind for the future. When you call on him the next time, he should be friendlier, more open. At least he will begin to realize that in case he needs you, you're there. Bear in mind that you may have to consistently call for a year or more on this type of prospect. Then all of a sudden he will buy. Your consistency and your planting the seed of doubt in previous interviews reap their reward.

Many times a customer will change his mind for all kinds of reasons: "Really don't like their present rep." "Personality conflict." "They changed terms and delivery on us once too often." "They've been taking us for granted too long." "Second time in a row they increased their price without even telling me." "They dropped their extra services." "Too many style changes."

Besides these six reasons there could be 66 more that will cause a buyer to turn his head in your direction. Be there! Be patient! I tell you it happens every day.

Tell your prospect that according to national statistics the average business loses 20 percent or more of its customers per year. This loss happens as naturally as the sun rises and sets. Don't tell him you know the average manager lasts only four years and five months before being replaced (my own research). It simply means you never know when you'll be looking at a new purchasing agent, or even a new owner (the average business lasts seven years, according to Dr. Robert McMurray of Chicago).

Your basic strategy is three-pronged. First, remember that 200 years of American history show that second suppliers are needed. Next, be patient—the odds favor you. Finally, keep calling. Let the purchaser know you are available.

Many buyers change suppliers at the beginning or the end of the year. So a lot of extra effort for new accounts is necessary in December and January. In their meetings, buyers make decisions on the basis of inventories, accounting department methods of recording and paying invoices, lines that "peter out" or outgrow their usefulness. Never fail to announce new products and new services in person and through the mails.

Incidentally, if you're not in the mail business, get into it! Fifty billion dollars a year in business is transacted through the mails. Every customer and prospect should get mail from you every month. Let the postman help you keep in touch. It helps get business from new customers, from old customers, and from those who buy infrequently. After you have planted the idea of a second (or first) supplier, your job is to cultivate that thought, as a gardener babies his seed.

SIX EASY WAYS TO KEEP IN TOUCH

1. Frequent personal calls.
2. Steady mail.
3. Occasional "hot specials."
4. Your own handwritten letter about market changes.
5. Occasional lunch.
6. Having the prospect test your new products.

You must use a strategy of continuous low-pressure contact. Sooner or later it will win for you when you need the extra business. Think of it! You can have dozens of new customers. This is really the business of business. The top strategist uses this method to pick up lots of new customers. He gets more than his share in what I call the annual million-dollar commission-and-bonus scramble. He knows there are plenty of orders just waiting for the salesman who does his home work. The alert, positive, aggressive salesman is not scared off by the squeak of the rocking chair. He zeros in on it!

While visiting a Weyerhauser office, I was pleased to see a huge board with some 12 company names on it and one statement: "We want these companies as steady customers!" The manager said: "We'll get them sooner or later—even if it takes three years!" I was truly impressed. Do you have a list of "wanted steady customers" for your territory? Are they posted in your office for all to see?

Another approach that has worked in the "I love our present supplier" situation is to ask the buyer, point blank, to fill you in on the supplier: his delivery schedules, terms, prices, extra services, rebates. You may even get him to tell it all in just one interview. After the interview, record the information as fast as you can. File the material for future use. You may use that very same information to sell Mr. Rocking Chair at a later date. It's possible you may be able to dislodge your competition one day with one small piece of information.

Make it known you're in the game for a long, long time. Short-term people may make temporary gains with underhanded methods, but if you stay in there for "the long, hard pull," you will pick up the pieces. When you hear: "Our present supplier is doing a good enough job," just remember basic human nature. Somewhere along the line, someone is going to stumble. If you went out of your way to "get yourself noticed" by a purchaser, you are in a good position to profit from the old supplier's mistakes.

In summary, your strategy should be:

- Tell the buyer in an alarmed way that it's poor business to deal with just a single supplier.
- Keep on calling in person or by letter. Keep the buyer posted on your new products and services.
- Have patience and understanding. Somewhere along the line, human nature will prevail. Someone will goof, and you will "clean up"!

You need superhuman patience in the "million-dollar scramble" for bonuses and commissions. But don't, repeat, don't sit patiently in your own rocking chair! You can't help someone out of his rocking chair from another rocker!

15
The Budget Blockade

Buyers often say: "It's not in the budget!" and brother, do they mean it! For generations, American businessmen have been taught to put one budget together and stick to it regardless of what comes along. So, my feeling is that this old worn-out notion is superimposed on everything in business—to the detriment of the enterprise itself!

I've partially solved this difficult situation and closed numerous sales by using a simple technique I used with Investors Diversified Services of Minneapolis, a very successful mutual fund company. The company actually wanted to train 80 of its salespeople but had no budget at the time, just a strong desire to train them. Then I asked the vice president I was dealing with: "Would your advertising department, or your promotion department, or your research department, or even your public relations department have an extra $12,000 they didn't spend this year? You know how budgets go: if they don't spend it, they lose it!" There was complete silence. He didn't stir, nor did I. I felt I had hit on a full or at least partial solution. Apparently the vice president did too, for he pardoned himself and left the room. He came back shortly and said: "I got half the $12,000 from the advertising department. You've made a sale if you'll bill the other half in February." Even if I had a budget problem of my own, I would have managed the billing delay!

Previously, I would have lost 100 percent in that situation. After the IDS episode, I began to polish and refine my approach to this budget problem. I even asked people if they had "miscellaneous budgets." It worked! I began to realize that no companies have sales or management training in their budgets, but I found that they all have advertising and promotion budgets. Also I discovered that they have "special budgets" of one kind or another: research and development, executive development, year-end and quarterly bonuses, and, of course, cash reserves. A large St. Paul company allowed executives to write checks on the spot as long as they were not over $2,500! They wrote these checks on "a special fund for bargain purchases or new product purchases." Man, was I excited! The discovery that companies had these various funds under different labels truly astonished me. For years I had been operating in the dark, barking up the wrong tree. I'd been plain incompetent. I started to figure out how to run around the old Budget Blockade.

Is it possible you are approaching prospective buyers incorrectly by expecting to do something that they consider impossible: screw up their budget? They just will not do that. But if you are not just like every other salesperson, you can alter your basic approach in a unique way. You can anticipate resistance and deliberately set the stage for a new type of negotiation. You start in by flatly admitting that you do not know if your proposition is in their budget at all, but you also bring out the fact that it may be possible to get it into another budget like research and development, or advertising, or

promotion, or miscellaneous. Ask the buyer for his help.
Don't try to sell him outright. Let him help you to the solution
that only he can find. This is truly the best way to sell
anything. Don't ever try to do all the work in any situation.
Just tell the buyer that you will work with him as a team to
solve his problem. If you try to do it by yourself, he will keep
the idea that he already has: that it's your problem, not his.
You have to get him out of the protection of that stupid
budget. You do this by conveying to him the idea that it is his
problem. So when you hear: "It's not in the budget," do these
things:

1. Smoothly explore the possibility that other departments
   in the company have the funds to cover your sale.
2. Gently condition his thinking by asking if advertising,
   promotion, research, education, or the like have the
   necessary funds.
3. Explain the togetherness principle, sincerely and tact-
   fully. Get the buyer to feel it is his problem, and help him
   want to solve it.

If, when you ask for funds from other departments, your
prospect scratches his head or smiles, you might just have
started the wheels rolling in his mind. Remember, he is a
purchasing agent. His job is to buy things or services, so he
naturally feels sorry if you walk out without a purchase order
or an okayed agreement.

If you sell high-cost items, you can be ready to run the
budget blockade if you have available reliable lenders who are
looking for an "in" with just about any top, growing company.
Many lenders love to loan out money for capital equipment
and other big purchases just to become second banks for new
customers.

The great Heinz Goldman gave as his definition of
selling: "Salesmanship is doing what the other fellow doesn't
do." This means an ordinary salesman can become extraordi-

nary if he'll only use his imagination and approach prospects not like a peddler but as one businessman to another. You're in business; your client is in business; you're equal! He is the buyer; you are the seller. When you approach a prospective buyer, three things are absolutely vital:

1. What he sees has to be good. That's you!
2. How he feels has to be good. You help him feel good!
3. What he hears has to be an answer to his prayers. You provide that answer!

Your prospective purchaser is filled with wants and desires. He knows he has to grow if he is to survive in his job. Charles Darwin's law of the survival of the fittest applies to him.

Don't fold when you hear, "It's not in the budget." Start differently if you expect to hear that remark, and of course, now you'll react differently. In summary:

• Be prepared to ask if other funds are available for new or bargain purchases.
• Press hard on the togetherness principle of solving the problem you just created for the buyer.
• Do something different. Provide a lender who doesn't mind being a company's second bank. Use your imagination to put the sale together.

Study your situation more. Are you just a salesman, a vendor who only wants to sell, or are you a businessman dealing with other businessmen?

William Henley said, "I am the master of my Fate! I'm the captain of my soul!" Thoreau said, "Our life is frittered away by detail. Simplify, simplify!"

Don Sheehan says, "Amen to Henley and Thoreau. As the captain of my soul, I cannot fritter away my time with details such as budgets that get in the way. As a businessman, I look for other funds that pave the way."

16
Close, Don't Edify!

You've given your full talk, and the prospect tells you, "I can't make a decision. You'll have to see Mr. Brown."

You may have just committed the basic error of giving your presentation without politely asking the prospect if, in case he likes the deal, he has the authority to make a financial decision on what is being presented.

They claim Samson killed thousands of people with the jawbone of an ass. Thousands of sales are lost daily through the "jawboning" of—er—salespeople who forget to qualify prospects. You may edify the prospects with your well-worded presentation, but if you do not qualify them, you have just wasted a speech! The mere fact that a prospect listens to you, nods agreement, and smiles means nothing if he or she lacks the authority to purchase.

If you find this out, either before or after your "spiel," ask the prospect to take you over and introduce you to "Mr. Brown" or "Ms. Smith." This gives you a small advantage. When one member of a firm introduces you to an officer, the impression is created that the company is interested in your offer. "Mr. Brown" is predisposed to think his firm is leaning your way.

It is also possible that the prospect's referring you to "Mr. Brown" is a form of passing the buck. Challenge his request that you see "Mr. Brown": "Does Mr. Brown have authority to make a financial decision?" Continue to ask him who does have the authority to make a decision. Some people will give you the go-around until you nail down who really is the buyer.

Here are some of the questions to ask:

1. Is it a committee?
2. Is it a department head?
3. Is it the general manager of the firm?
4. Is it the president of the company?
5. Is it the home office in New York City?
6. Who makes the financial decision?

Learn this rule right now: don't just give talks for the sake of talking. You'll wear yourself out. Winners don't just talk for talk's sake. Within a minute or two after your introduction, protect yourself by asking: "If what you see and hear is what you want, can you make a financial decision on it?" It's either "yes" or "no." "Maybes" are not good enough! This tactic has saved me hundreds of hours of frustration and brought me bigger sales and commissions than ever before.

For a salesperson to present a product to an unqualified buyer is foolhardy. Anytime you have an unknown prospect in front of you, you're on dangerous ground. If you expect a decision in your favor, you must take the time to determine whether he can or can't make a financial decision.

It takes guts, determination, tact, strategy; but the qualification of the prospect must take place before a presentation is made. No one gains when two or three presentations have been made. You needlessly double and triple your efforts when you avoid the financial authority question. If you do not ask this question in the first three to five minutes of the interview, you've already lost. You are not really selling; you're just telling.

Be suspicious of the type of buyer who is silent. He may not have much to do and is looking for entertainment. He would prefer to go to the ball game. The company won't stand for that, but the buyer knows that if he looks busy, no one will complain. So he listens to you—or pretends to listen. Check on his buying authority even sooner. You're a salesman, not an entertainer. In summary:

- Ask all unknown or new buyers: "If you like what you see and hear, do you have the authority to buy?"
- When he asks you to "see Mr. Brown," have him take you over for a formal introduction.
- Start right! Qualify the prospect within three to five minutes—or you lose.

17

Don't Wait Your Turn—Sell Now!

What do you do when you find your prospect will be listening to presentations from two or more salespeople? You simply fool everyone! You don't make a presentation! Rather than talking to the prospect, you ask questions—a hundred if necessary. Tell the buyer you are busy as a salesperson because your company is trying to fill its orders. Tell him that you need the answers to dozens of questions.

Let's face it, if he's talking to one other salesman, your chances of closing are about 50 percent. If he's talking to two other salesmen, your odds are down to 33 percent. So don't do what the others do! Don't give a high-powered, standard pitch. No! Stop the show! Ask him who, what, when, where, how, and why. Ask what he'll do with your product, where he'll use it, how he'll use it, who will use it, what results he wants, what kind of money he wants to pay, his terms, his delivery requirements. Ask if he's interested in warranties and guarantees. How much after-sale service and follow-up does he expect? If you can think of any more questions, ask them!

Write it all down on a checkoff sheet. Then look at the buyer (because he will usually want it all) and tell him it's quite in order. You can't promise him anything until you've conferred with your headquarters. Thank him for his time. Leave him hanging. Tell him you'll get back to him as soon as you've cleared all this with your company.

Now stop and analyze your strategy. You're not in there begging for an order. No, you're in there now on a different basis: businessman to businessman. You are making this prospect sell himself! You are even telling him you don't know if you can handle him as a customer. This twist, as a rule, usually kills second- or third-party salesmen. It takes a certain amount of guts and planning, but it pays off like crazy. Too many salesmen walk in there desperate just to get an order. No! Bug off! Play hard to get. Prospects are human beings. They always want something they can't have.

Yes, deliberately tell people that you want to think about their needs, that you want to go over things with your people. Make them want your deal. It's a ploy of the rich—and a good way to get rich.

I'm here to tell you they come running to you! So stall. Don't be overanxious to sell when one or more salesmen got in ahead of you. Force buyers to come to you. Don't let them dictate to you and force you to the wall. If you do, you usually end up "buying the business," which means an exchange of dollars with neither dignity nor money left in the deal for you.

It is undignified to wait in line. It is also time-consuming, so you must turn things around. Make the customer stand in line! He won't know what hit him—or his pocketbook.

18
The Confused Buyer

When a buyer seems confused, you may get no reaction at all. For instance, if the buyer takes notes, he may be a "shopper." On the other hand, you could have overtalked the product. You may have confused him with too many items. If he's not with you, *stop!* Start all over by asking the buyer: "What is it that's causing you to hesitate? Are there points that I've made that have caused you to hesitate?" Ask if you talked too fast or too low or if something is unclear to him. Silence is a must here on your part. Letting him talk is one of the few chances you have here, so shut up. Yes, shut up and sell! Things are not going right, but your suggestions may just help you save the situation.

   Did he invite you to his place, or did you invite yourself? There is a difference! If he invited you, you have the advantage, and you must use that advantage when you detect a neutral reaction. Restate the purpose of the call. This is basic in a business transaction. What's the purpose of the interview? Is it to gather information, to inspect, to learn, to become

acquainted, to size each other up for character and total
buying and selling potential, or is the purpose of the interview
to arrive at a positive or negative decision?

Courtesy rules the roost. The purpose of a sale is to
please. You get no reaction when a buyer is confused. One of
four things is wrong:

1. You're off the track. You're not talking about what the
   buyer wanted to hear. You're talking to please yourself,
   not the buyer.
2. Your presentation is of such poor quality that the buyer is
   having a hard time following you. He's too polite to tell
   you that you're in an advanced state of the mumbles and
   not hitting home with him.
3. The buyer is disappointed in what she's hearing. She
   expected more. Her disappointment shows in her lack of
   reaction.
4. The buyer is trying to put all the pieces together, and his
   confused look and lack of reaction have no meaning to the
   final result of the sale. His reaction could be only
   temporary.

Your best approach is to rely on politeness, patience, and
helpfulness. The situation is not promising. You need to keep
your cool to give yourself every opportunity to regain his
attention and interest. Study your prospect. Every change is
important. It can signal either his pleasure or his displeasure.

In summary, be alert to this type of buyer in the future
and try to handle him in the following manner:

• Watch the shopper who takes notes. You know you'll have
  to get a second interview to sell.
• Be careful not to "overtalk" the product.
• At the first signs of confusion or nonreaction, stop and ask
  questions as to what is causing the buyer to hesitate.

- Shut up and let the buyer talk.
- Review the purpose of the interview.
- Find out if you are completely off the track.
- Assess your presentation. Was it poor?
- Is the buyer disappointed in what he's hearing? Then change the subject.
- Is the buyer quiet because she's trying to fit the big picture together to see if you fit? Ask her.
- Be patient; be polite; be helpful.

19

The Different Company

"Our company is different. I don't think you can help us!" is a most immature remark; yet many a buyer makes it. He's probably a guy in his late twenties or thirties. It's a naive statement, because he's probably not the real buyer anyway! So I humor him and say, "Well, if I do help you, there will be an extra charge, because you probably are different, so it will be harder to help you." You say this with a smile. Then you turn the tables on him pleasantly and diplomatically. He's already displayed his lack of open-mindedness and his narrow provincial thinking, so do just the opposite of what he expects from you—in a friendly way.

In a cordial voice, ask him if you could show him how to make extra profits for his company even though it is different. Could he make a financial decision on your product or service? Chances are, nine out of ten, he can't. So why bother? Find the man in his company who can.

Let's face it: most people think their company is different, but all I've seen in my years is a terrible sameness in failing companies. Only 16 percent of all managers can generate acceptable profits.

If you're truly convinced your offer is sound, then all companies are potential buyers, from the mom and pop grocery to giants such as IBM, Bell Telephone, or General Motors. Don't let the buyer get to you on this point of not needing help. One company in 50 is profitable. The average worker in the United States lasts four years, seven months. Don't fall for buyers who have drummed up their grand behavior before you arrive. Your chances of closing such a purchaser are very small. Be prepared to move fast! You're better off looking for new prospects. When you run up to a real mud hole, you are better off turning around and finding a different road.

In summary, if you hear, "Our company is different":

- Realize your chances are slim.
- Ask the buyer if he can make a final decision in case you can still help his company.
- Size him up to see if he's worth the effort!

20
Five Minutes to Sell

How do you close when a prospect says, "You've got five minutes"? This beautiful greeting is given to salesmen 1,000 times an hour all over America. The inexperienced salesman can only sweat in panic when faced with a five-minute deadline. He cannot score. But the old pro will use it to his advantage. In fact, I welcome the statement, because it tells me exactly where I stand with the buyer. Need I remind you that 98 percent of the time the buyer is thinking only of himself, certainly not about you?

Try this. Counter his limitation by giving him only part of your presentation, and make it a juicy warm-up story to whet his appetite to hear more. Then cut him off and use your remaining two minutes to set up a future appointment to tell your complete story! Cut him short by sticking to his five minutes. Under no circumstances stay longer. He deliberately tried to intimidate you. Now you intimidate him!

Take my advice. You must be in control of the sale if you are ever going to close. Punish the buyer deliberately by not telling the rest of the story. Whether you make him mad at you or hungry to hear more, it has to be done to protect your own dignity. Study the buyer. Is he the type of person you want to do business with in the next five years? Can you live with his personality? Is he your type? Does he fit the mold of the high-volume, high-profit type of buyer? Does he have the potential to yield more profits for you? Or will you continue to have to submit yourself to more domineering? You lose if you do!

In the South St. Paul area, a buyer in the water purifier business hit me with the "five-minute" act. After sizing him up and talking to him for four or five minutes, I stood up and said pleasantly that I did not feel I'd care to do business with him and smilingly thanked him for listening. In my car I gently patted myself on the back, because the buyer "smelled like trouble" and was bound to have personality conflicts with me or any other self-respecting salesmen. Basically, the man was a bully. Who, in this day and age, has to put up with that behavior when he has the whole world to see?

Play hard to get! Yes, sometimes I deliberately refuse to give my presentation, stating it would be an injustice to both of us. I tell the buyer, "Your profits this year could be at stake in this conversation. I need at least 30 minutes to present my proposition professionally or else I excuse myself." Either you'll get the 30-minute hearing or he'll accept a later appointment.

Under no circumstances be forced into doing the impossible: making a serious presentation in just five minutes. Don't do something foolish because of a foolish request.

Your position as a salesman must always be one of strength. I always bring my pocket secretary and my big 8½" × 11" calendar. I lay it on a prospect's desk so he can see it, and I casually tell him that I'm 98 percent booked for the next six months. He sees this in black, white, and red. I circle in red all my daily bookings—not only for my benefit, but for the prospect's as well. Red excites a bull. It can also excite the guy who gives it to you.

The moment you are cowed by his bullying, you are finished with that sale.

In summary, here's what you do the next time you get that old "five-minute" business:

- Warm up the prospect for three minutes; then use two minutes to ask for a future appointment.
- Ask right off for a future appointment by stating that you'll need at least 30 minutes to be fair to both of you; then stand up and be ready to leave.
- Walk out after sizing him up and ask yourself if you really want to do business with him. Will he grow?
- Watch your position. Either you control the sale or you lose it. Don't let people lord it over you.

21

Your Bag of Closes

If you can't close, you can't sell. So learn the bag of closing tricks in this chapter and you'll be well on your way to becoming a master at closing sales.

CALL-BACKS

Don't call back on a prospect just to ask him for an order to give him more information. Give him more ways to save or earn money. Even if you call back a dozen times, don't tell—sell!

When you phone a prospect, don't ask him if he decided to purchase. Give him more information and get him to make an appointment. When it comes to closing, the first move is always up to the salesman. Rarely will a prospect jump up and demand that you take an order. You must take the first step, even when the prospect comes to you. Expect to make the first move yourself. The only thing I can think of right now that people will usually buy without your asking is trouble, and that's free in most places.

SMALL GIFTS

To close faster you should use small gifts to break the ice. Paul Stafford, working as an estimator for Cervin Electric in Minneapolis, upped his closing average in two years from 50 percent to 71 percent simply by offering the prospect a quarter-pound box of Fanny Farmer candy. The 21 percent increase in sales raised his profits like crazy. The candy cost him only 80 cents, but this kind gesture made his customers want him to sell!

SPECIALS

Does your company use introductory offers, close-out items, end-of-line items, or factory seconds? If so, present these items first when you talk to a prospect. This usually warms him up, and it enables you to sell other items to improve your profit. One type of purchaser, the Cherry Picker, may want only the specials. But the Cherry Picker, glowing with elation over getting "something for nothing," is in a perfect mood to listen when you tell him he's low on other items.

Specials can be used to break into a new company or to get the ball rolling with a tough buyer.

CHANGE BAIT

Discounts and extended payment terms are excellent tools for earning more business. It's just good salesmanship to lay all the options out to the buyer so he can choose one or all your "money closes." A good business is constantly on the alert to buy better. Your prime job is to use these savings as leverage to get orders. That's really why alert businessmen come up with quantity discounts, 2 percent cash discounts, and longer pay plans: to get the buyer to take action now. Hundreds of salesmen have waited for the prospect to "mail or call them an order." They are still waiting, because prospects seldom call. Ninety-five percent of all orders are lost forever simply because salesmen didn't use the right tools. Waiting for a buyer to call is like waiting for the *Queen Mary* to dock. It just won't happen.

The biggest closers are the best planners! They're system people. They do it just like we put a man on the moon—step by step. They think big and, after they qualify a prospect, have enough guts to ask for the order. They truly have the desire to win!

Like the suitor who really wants the girl, you pop the question right now! The suitor shows the girl a sparkling diamond. You offer your client a discount or a longer pay plan.

The girl say, "Oh yes, honey!"

Your client says, "Say! That's an offer I can't refuse!"

TESTIMONIAL LETTERS

The testimonial-letter close is worth easily $100,000 in commissions. Everyone likes a story, and it is a thousand times more exciting one when you can back it up with the author's stationery and his signature. Here's how I did it. I put on an intensive sales course for the Future Homes Company of New York Mills, Minnesota. The president, Jim Larson, hired me to help his 25 salesmen sell more houses. He told me how much each of his eight sales centers had to sell. I asked him what would really please him. He said, "If we could sell 100 homes in a month, everybody would be thrilled."

We did sell the 100 homes, but, better still, in the four months of the training program, we increased sales 97 percent. Jim Larson gladly put the 97 percent sales increase on paper, and I use his letter all over America. Conservatively, the letter has been worth $100,000 in extra commissions to me in two years' time.

Can you use success stories in your business?

THE EXPERT'S TESTIMONY

Bring an expert with you to help you close. I've done it! Call a particularly difficult prospect and tell him you have an expert with you whom you'd like him to meet. When we introduced Ajax Cleanser, my boss, H. J. Shea, would come with me to show the sudsing and cleansing action. All he used was a milk bottle to prove that Ajax Cleanser actually was a cleanser with sudsing power. He helped me convince merchants that the cleanser was selling all over the country and would work in hard-water areas.

The demonstration, plus the voice of authority (he was a man of 45 then and a really cool guy), did the trick! In two years we had distribution in 96 percent of the outlets, plus we were number one in the marketplace.

FIFTEEN-DAY TRIAL

For one solid year I attempted to sell my cassette tapes through the mail, with little success. In fact, I lost thousands of dollars mailing thousands of pieces of mail. Then I used research! It proved that people would try my many products when I told them they could return them within 15 days and receive a full refund. I HEADLINED that offer in my next mailing and promptly sold $5,000 worth of tapes—and there were *no* refunds! I'll recheck my refunds at the $20,000 level, but I expect them to be from 2 percent to 5 percent. Not bad for a product that was a loser!

SATISFACTION GUARANTEED

Many products and services are purchased on the basis of "satisfaction guaranteed." My experience tells me you can have a buy-back of 5 percent to 20 percent, so be prepared. If you make the offer, spell out the time limit and other conditions. I used to sell courses that way and generally got requests for refunds around Christmas time. People needed the money then.

It does work, especially on a new product, but, again, be most careful in writing out and explaining your guarantees so there's no misunderstanding. Though you can make 100 sales and buy back only five, I suggest you use it for new products and services only. On the whole, the technique has a good business-getting history.

PURE LARCENY

Recently I sold two companies on bringing me to the San Francisco area, simply by telling them, "You can cut your travel expenses in half if you book me the same week another company is using me." It worked. I set up both talks at my convenience simply because the saving of several hundred dollars was too strong a temptation to resist. I call this share-the-expense offer the Larceny Close. The desire to get something for nothing is so strong, it pushes your prospect into a decision in your favor.

Can you get two companies to split shipping costs? Split service costs? There is nothing wrong with this, but getting something for nothing appeals to the larcenous streak in all of us. The Master Tempter sees to that!

This is probably the only time Old Nick works in the interest of the "good guy"!

CLOSE WITH STATISTICS

You can use numbers to close. I've made thousands of sales using a variety of researched facts to close individuals and groups. For nearly 20 years I've consistently scored a 2 percent response with a monthly letter to 2,000 to 8,000 businesspeople in a given area:

Dear Sir:

DO YOU EXPECT TO BE IN BUSINESS THE NEXT 5 YEARS? The odds are not encouraging! Did you know that 75 out of every 100 new businesses fail within five years? Only one company in 20 makes the profits it should. Up to 50 percent of your present employees could turn over in the next 18 months. The average life of many businesses is only four years. Sixty-eight percent of your present customers will quit doing business with you this year because someone in your company was discourteous to them!

The letter includes an invitation to a breakfast or dinner event. At the meeting I write on a blackboard 20 cases of business failure. I point out that 92 percent fail because of poor management and that the average manager lasts four and one-half years. Then I sell them on one of my training courses on sales and management. Does it work? These "free meal" meetings have helped me make over 20,000 closes! This is not bad, especially when you consider that my breakfast sales pitches are made at 7 A.M. Statistical closes are most effective on groups. I could write a book on group closes!

CONSIGN, THEN DEMONSTRATE

Sometimes you can combine closings, as I did when I put together the consignment-and-demonstration close. Osco Drug of St. Cloud and Rochester, Minnesota, accepted from me a consignment of several thousand cleaning pads. I told the manager, "Let me put them in on consignment and demonstrate the pads to the public on Friday nights and all day Saturday." He accepted! How could they lose? So from 6 P.M. to 10 P.M. on two Friday nights and from 9 A.M. to 9 P.M. on two Saturdays, I sold and sold. I dressed in a white tuxedo and stovepipe hat. I really did a business—and I was not supposed to be a businessman! I was attending St. John's University at Collegeville, Minnesota, as a senior, but this sale helped put me in business. It convinced me I could close and close! I really made outstanding commissions in St. Cloud, just 12 miles from St. John's. I sold out all my merchandise in two days and two evenings. They were full days and full evenings, but they were full of success.

Everything was full! My heart with contentment; my friends, with envy; and, best of all, my pockets with hard cash—really something for a college kid.

THE NEW PRODUCT

"New" is not the only magic word in the dictionary, but newspaper people like it. If it weren't such an exciting word, a lot of editors and reporters would have to get out and look for work. When I introduced Florident, Colgate's household deodorant, I carried a sample wherever I called. I would set the container on the supermarket or wholesaler's counter. Then I uncapped it and very lightly scented the air. Every customer I called on smelled this new scent of this new product. The only thing old about the whole deal was that my customers responded in a manner as ancient as sin. They went crazy over something new. About all I had to do was to close by convincing them that this new product was also a high-profit item.

USE THE DOOR KNOB

I was trying to sell my training class to the La Haas Corporation of Mendota, Minnesota. Working with Frank Hasselman, I gave him my usual story and tried to get an order to train 15 people on his premises. He was interested, but not interested enough. He put me off: "I'll make a decision next week."

While standing in his parking lot, a small rage was burning inside me. I said to myself, "I should have sold Frank." It was almost a chant. I said, "I should have made that sale." I went directly back and knocked on Frank's office door with double determination. Back in his office, I stood there with fire in my eyes and voice: "Frank, you and your people should start that course next Tuesday night." He stood up, dialed his intercom, talked to his controller, Ernie, and told him, "Make out a check to Sheehan. We are going next Tuesday night."

Frank walked out with me to the door, looked me in the eye, and said, "I'm glad you came back; I'm afraid I would have kept putting off that decision."

I must caution you to be 100 percent sincere on this close. The prospect must gain in some special way by his immediate purchase.

GUIDE THEM IN

You literally have to guide people to your place of business, show them how to use your services or product. People have terrific fears that they'll fail in using your product or service, or worse yet, that they'll suffer from embarrassment in front of fellow workers or the family.

I closed a man on the phone on buying my class, but I had to spend 20 minutes more on Ma Bell's squawk box instructing him how to find the hotel where I would hold the meeting. It was in a part of town unfamiliar to him, and it was a winter night. My patience in instructing him on how to get to class worked. He showed up with his check in hand.

DEMONSTRATE AND SELL

Day in and day out, demonstration closes sell more cars, more motorcycles, washers, driers, more machinery of all kinds. Curt Cervin of Cervin Electric said to me, "If your course is so good, show me just two extra closes that will help my estimator get business and I'll buy your courses." I did, and he bought my demonstration on the spot! Incidentally, one of the closing aids I told him about, a quarter-pound box, helped his leading salesman, Paul Stafford, leap from a two-year closing average of 50 percent to 71 percent. Was he happy! Curt Cervin, even happier, later enrolled four more people in my class.

All I did was demonstrate the proper use of quarter-pound boxes of candy. They should be used to put a bit of fat on your customer and a whole lot more in your pocketbook.

HELP FROM THE SIDELINES

In the trading area of every city are key people who rule the local business roost. A nod from one of them is gold in your pockets. This key person could be a banker, a manufacturer, a distributor, or just anyone who's big on the scene.

When Wes Fesler resigned as head football coach at the University of Minnesota, he joined Investors Diversified Services in Minneapolis. After he attended my seminars, Fesler helped me sell more than 200 IDS salesmen on taking my course on salesmanship.

George Mikan, also of Minneapolis, and Mr. Basketball of the last 50 years, not only attended my seminars but, as did Wes Fesler, influenced hundreds of people to use my training courses. Successful people like to help the up-and-coming guy.

OFFER A FREE SERVICE

Irv Lundeen of Paper Supply, Minneapolis, invited me in to talk to his salesmen about a program that I was offering. Irv had taken the Dale Carnegie course from me previously and was completely satisfied. My purpose in coming into his company and offering a free talk was to get something else going. Sure enough, two of Irv's employees enrolled in my next class. As boss, Irv was reluctant to push anyone into something, but my "free service" or "sample talk" got me two sales.

USE YOUR EGO PROPERLY

You can assert yourself—use your ego to close. Your self-esteem, your pride, your self-image should all be used to get a close. This drive you're on, the challenge to get the job done, should be nurtured and kept sharp. Your ego will help you get a close, but you need to temper your ego with empathy, the ability to put yourself in the prospect's shoes and suffer along with him. Too much ego—self-esteem that's not balanced with empathy—will lose sales for you.

The great Earl Nightingale of "Strongest Secret" fame talked of the empathy-ego balance years ago. His ideas are valid today. You need ego to sell, but you also need to counter it with understanding. Ego must not get in the way of your sale.

USE A CO-WORKER TO CLOSE BY PHONE

When you are in a closing situation and the sale seems to be bogging down, just pick up the phone and call your manager. After dialing the number, tell your client you want him to "speak to an official from my company." When your manager answers, tell him you are "with the Smiths" and hand the receiver to the prospect to talk to your boss. This two-on-one selling impresses the prospect and gets excellent closing results. Be sure, however, to see to it that your manager is going to be in if you plan on using this strategy. All your manager has to do is reassure the prospect that he's doing the right thing.

USE GUTS TO CLOSE

Examine for a minute the word "guts." It should remind you of the slogan: "Get You To Sign." People hate to say no to people. Yes is so much easier to say. Since you are a "seller," not a "speller," you won't have too much trouble with the "U" standing for "you." I've sold millions of dollars worth of merchandise, wholesale and retail, direct, tangibles, intangibles, services—you name it. It all comes down to your staying power with a customer—your *guts!*

I called on E. B. Crabtree Company of Minneapolis once every three months for seven years. I finally sold them. Figuring my commission on the basis of 28 calls in seven years, I convinced myself that long-range selling pays off. If I can sell accounts like that every seven years, I can retire seven years earlier.

BUY THREE—GET ONE FREE!

Offering one free item for three purchased is an excellent way to get good volume quickly if your prices are right. It's good for you and good for your customer. It fills the pipe line and gets fast distribution for you, whether it's wholesale, retail, or direct. Let's face it, everybody likes a bargain, whether he or she is a consumer or a commercial user.

In a slow season I offered this deal to customers who put people in my classes. I had nearly full classes while everyone else was running half empty.

GET HELP FROM A CUSTOMER

It dawned on me one day that if I brought with me a satisfied furniture dealer to make a call on the North St. Paul Chamber of Commerce, I might do better. I asked the furniture dealer to go along. He proudly accepted. Point blank I asked him what he would say to the Chamber secretary. He said, "Every chamber member in this town could benefit from your closing techniques!" That was good enough for me. My friend said just exactly that to the secretary, who quickly set up a class for 25 people!

Do you have a satisfied customer who will make calls with you? I bet you do!

The customer need not come in person. I sold a training class to a company in the paper business by just standing up, walking to the phone, and calling Midway Ford in St. Paul for the owner, Jerome O'Brian Slawick. I told Jerry I was talking to a paper company and asked him to tell my prospect how he liked the three classes I had put on for Jerry's company. He and the prospect talked for 20 minutes. After a few minutes, I walked back in the room (I purposely went out to get a glass of water). My prospect looked at me and said, "I'll take it."

This telephone technique has resulted in tens of thousands of dollars in commissions for me.

MAKE IT WITH A MINOR POINT

I sold a Twin Cities manufacturer on putting on a managers'
class for 15 of his key managers by making just a minor point.
The total cost of the program was $6,000. We had talked for
one hour on his committing 15 people to a class on his
premises. However, my client said: "I cannot commit myself
today until I talk to my brother, who is my partner." I was
getting nowhere fast. So I said, "Will you want the seminar on
your own premises or somewhere else?" He promptly took me
to a room where the meetings could be held at 7 A.M., but he
said regular employees come in at 8 A.M., which would
interrupt my two-hour class.

That was my break! I told him I'd pick up the bill on
holding the class in a nearby hotel where there'd be no
interruptions if he agreed right that day. He did! He
immediately talked to his brother, who gave the go-ahead.
The additional cost to me of $160 for coffee and toast was well
worth the $6,000 close.

You will find many other minor points to distract your
client from his real reason for hesitation.

THE NO-LITERATURE CLOSE

For seven years I have not given out a piece of literature!

Most salesmen make a big mistake here. When the selling
gets tough, they give literature to the prospect. I figured out
that all it does is get the prospect off the hook. He feels secure
with the literature. He feels he "knows it all" with the
literature. It literally satiates him when he tucks that brochure
under his arm. The only man who wins is the printer. He gets
paid, you lose the prospect nine times out of ten. When he
asks for literature, I show him a copy but tell him it's my only

sample. I do not give it to him. If I'm at my office, I show him a big book with testimonials in it.

The only time I give literature is when someone writes for it, and that is about three times a year.

Next time someone asks for a brochure, show the "only one you're got." Normally, that will satisfy him.

THE REFERRAL CLOSE

I attempted to close a big grocery client of mine on putting on a class for him, his five store managers, and their assistants. He liked the idea, but at the last minute, for some reason or other, turned it down. I graciously thanked him for his consideration and began to leave. I had picked up my briefcase and papers, put my coat on, and was ready to exit. With my hand on the door, I said, "Do you happen to know anyone else in the grocery field who has talked to you about training their managers?"

Without hesitation he supplied a name. The referral came quickly, because it was to a man who was not a competitor and who did business outside of my first client's territory. This referral put 30 people into a motivation class—nearly three times what I attempted to sell my regular client. When I reviewed my records for that year, that referral sale proved to be the most profitable sale of the year! I didn't have to advertise for it. I didn't have to pay a cent for it. All I had to do was have enough sense to ask for it.

It is always good sense to ask for help when you need it.

THE BUYER-PROTECTION-PLAN CLOSE

You can use the buyer-protection-plan close on the "walk-outs" or the ones you'd call "impossibles." Though you've done almost everything, without being able to close, it is still not time to panic. Tell the buyer as he's leaving, "Have you heard of our buyer protection plan? Here's how it works. You give me a deposit today on that merchandise, and if the merchandise increases in price, I'll give it to you at the lower price. In addition to that, I'll write on the purchase agreement that you have 72 hours to return this merchandise if you're not completely satisfied, and I'll give you your money back. Now, doesn't that sound fair to you?"

People can be closed with this 72-hour close. Incidentally, only 10 percent return merchandise, according to the many salesmen who have used the plan. To look at it positively, 90 percent of the sales stick! However, use the 72-hour close only as a last resort. It takes longer than I like to deliver, and it commits you to a lot of "goodies"; but if you need it to close, use it. It can be a beautiful close for people who retail big-ticket items, and has great potential for many other products and services.

USE RESEARCH

Many local libraries keep records on business firms that started in the community. These records go back 50 years or longer in some cases. Quotes from these histories have earned me close after close. One Minneapolis auto parts company was utterly amazed that I knew "so much history" of the company—when it started, who founded it, what it sold, its current officers. I had told the prospect, "Your dominance in this market since 1921 means you keep your people trained to the teeth on the newer techniques of selling." He enrolled 22 salespeople in a company class and kept enrolling them for years after.

Prospects are pleasantly surprised and happy that you recognize their history. If a library isn't handy, stop off and get information from gas stations, other companies, friends, or right out of the literature in the company's waiting room. Prospects themselves will volunteer information. Ask, "How did the firm get started in this business?" Then sit back and listen. How they love to talk about themselves!

It really doesn't matter how you "research" them, as long as you close your deal.

THE MAIL FOLLOW-UP CLOSE

There are thousands of extra sales waiting for you if you take the time and trouble to (1) keep track of people who turn you down on a sale and (2) request a future contact. The temptation is to destroy prospect cards when you are forced to record "contact in 60 days" or "see next fall." There are legitimate reasons why people are unable to purchase when you want them to buy. A letter or a call to these people will result in 20 percent or more additional business you'd never get otherwise. This means one in five will purchase.

One evening I wrote full-page, handwritten letters to five prospects in Rochester, Minnesota, who still had not signed up for my training course. I knew one out of the five would buy. That meant I would get an actual $60 in commission per letter. The 20 percent figure fits this realistic formula: 75 percent of all sales are made on the first call, 20 percent on the second call, and 5 percent on the third. These are, of course, general percentages, so other products or services may modify the 75-20-5 figures, but for me it has worked wonders.

My letter merely tells the reader the time, date, and place of my next course and that he is cordially invited to attend the explanatory meeting as my personal guest. Ninety percent of those who accept are converted to cash sales.

Check your own follow-up system to see how many extra sales you can get out of the mail. That extra study of your follow-up performance could bring you the thousands of dollars so many salesmen throw away.

NEW CUSTOMERS WITH CARLOADS!

A special Ajax Cleanser package was offered by my company, so I talked to the owner of the Little Falls, Minnesota, Wholesale Grocery about purchasing merchandise on the carload basis. Once I landed the carload deal, I could work a five-county area and offer the cleanser to mechants at a reduced price. The idea was to stress to all merchants: "Here's a second supplier in your area who can be counted on for service, and he is up to date on the latest merchandise specials." It worked! The wholesaler bought a 40,000-pound box car of Ajax Cleanser!

You help yourself when you help others!

I went out and worked from morning to night to sell that carload of merchandise before it even arrived. I told local merchandisers that the wholesaler wanted to be a "second supplier" and was offering this merchandise to prove he was "as modern as the next guy."

I made sure each order was signed by the dealer and returned to the wholesaler to show him what I had done. He called his wife over and could hardly believe his eyes. He wanted to hire me to sell for him! But here's the punch line of the story: I sold him another 40,000-pound carload of Ajax. That year I won an Ajax gold plate from our New Jersey office for having sold 120 percent of my quota. Only a handful of people have received this nationwide award.

Can you go out and do the same with some wholesaler and move a lot of merchandise at the same time? My annual bonus for the year was a handsome check, plus a gold plate. My boss told me I was the highest-paid salesman in the district. His compliment spurred me on more than ever.

THE THREE R CLOSE

This is a beauty! You'll do thousands of extra dollars of business using it. Most big department stores use it effectively. It's simply stating in your advertising that you'll:

Refund the purchase price if the buyer is not satisfied,
Repair the article if defective, or
Replace the article with the same thing or another one.

Most consumers love it. Although some misuse it, in the long run, both the company and the consumer gain when you use the magnificent Three R Close.

The White Company, a building supply dealer, uses it in Minnesota very effectively by offering to pick up and credit any merchandise not sold by the buyer within 30 days after delivery. This helps get the merchandise in and displayed. The owner, John White, claims it helps him make those vital first-round sales.

THE COCKY CLOSE

Assume your client will buy. Your assumption will get through to the buyer. This is an easy close and one of the very best, but you must act out your part.

As you develop skill as a salesman, you won't really be cocky. You will know what you're doing.

THE SELLING SPURT

Whenever you're "hot," stay hot by continuing to sell. My father drummed this into my head at an early age. He explained it this way: "All of a sudden everything you do seems to click. It means that your head is synchronized just right. The trick is to milk everything you can out of the situation."

How true and sound that advice is! Working for the Colgate Company, I set a district record by writing 17 orders in 18 calls in one day. I got up at 5 A.M. to drive 70 miles to my first call. By the time I had breakfast and approached my first prospect it was 7:45 A.M. The grocer was in and didn't seem to mind my selling and closing him by 8 A.M. He bought a good order. No one was around to bother us, so I was off and running at a good clip. By 10 A.M. I'd written four orders!

I decided then and there that I was going for a record that day. I actually kept the motor in my car running, skipped lunch, coffee breaks, and dinner. By 8 P.M. I had written 17 orders in 18 calls: an all-time record for me and the district.

I had my dinner by 8:50 P.M. and ate with that all-American victory smile on my face. My district manager was stunned, and the company's monthly bulletin carried the headline: RECORD: 17 ORDERS IN ONE DAY.

The plain truth of the matter is that the typical salesman averages fewer than two and one-half calls per day. Industrial salesmen are supposed to make five calls per day. Two things, then, can be learned here:

1. When you're hot, skip everything else. Keep on selling and closing hour after hour.
2. "Burn in" a lot of calls. When you're hot, double, triple your exposure and keep your cool! To set an all-time record, you must be ready to set it. Then act and keep acting until you've had your biggest day!

THE SURPRISE ATTACK

To get a sale, you often can use the unusual—and sometimes with amusing results. I was trying to sell Rudy Boschwitz, president of a 50-location chain of a do-it-yourself business, on using my training course. Mr. Boschwitz pioneered the do-it-yourself concept in the Midwest. I sent him a telegram: "Dear Rudy, I'm ready! —Don Sheehan." He sent one back: "Dear Don, I'm not! —Rudy."

We both live in the same city, and we could have easily phoned each other. Yet for novelty's sake we sent telegrams. You can do the same. Incidentally, Rudy later became a big booster of mine, a United States Senator, and an excellent customer.

Always use Special Delivery letters. You need speed. Besides, Special Delivery puts you in a different class. People notice you more when you have Special Delivery written all over your letter. Mailgrams are also effective in informing and motivating buyers. I like to use 13 10¢ stamps to put on the face of an envelope. John White, president of White's Inc., Minneapolis, received one of my letters. When he looked at all the stamps on my letter, he not only bought a course for himself, but arranged a class for all his people. My method of closing impressed him.

Spend a little money. Please understand, you literally have to buy closes. Telegrams, Special Delivery letters, and small gifts all gain you a favorable impresssion with the buyer They are excellent ploys to gain an order. No tricks—just plain niceties. These are ideas that get the selling job done. So use any strategy as long as it's legal and ethical.

THE SUPER CLOSE

I once sold a druggist on selling a box of soap for a nickel and told him I would get him on the front page of his newspaper. I then furnished the publisher with perfume that would mix with ink. The happy publisher put a box on the front page: "Our paper is perfumed for the first time in history—see the drug ad on page 9." I sold the merchant 100 cases. He sold out all the 14,400 bars by noon. He needed a traffic officer in front of his store to keep cars moving!

MY FAVORITE CLOSE

I have a favorite close I use on prospects who call me up and want to see me about a program for their salespeople or for themselves. After introductions are over, I say to the prospect, "Suppose you like me, my course, and my low tuition. Suppose you like everything. Are you ready to buy today?" It works like crazy on the prospect who is "hot to trot." It takes far fewer words than the usual pitch, and you don't gamble away your prospect because of too much verbiage (a word which almost rhymes with garbage).

Most salesmen feel they can seduce a prospect by simply talking, talking, talking. Rarely does overtalking help. In fact, it quickly turns off a good prospect, because he feels he's being ignored.

Would you rather be talked at than listened to?

In Minot, North Dakota, I met a housing salesman who was really good. He regularly sold more than 125 mobile homes a year. These houses run from $6,000 to $36,000, so they are big-ticket items. When prospects walk into his sales center, this expert closer asks: "Are you here to buy a house today?" This rather curt, blunt opening statement is really a closing statement. He literally starts with a close! No wonder he sells so many homes. Do you have the courage to use statements like that? Believe me, starting with the close gave me a worldwide reputation with another organization. It sells and sells. So challenge prospects right off by a close. Here it is again: "Suppose, Mr. Prospect, that you like me, my product, my low price, everything about this. Are you ready to purchase today?" Or, like the ace in North Dakota, "Are you here to buy a home today?" I dare you to experiment. Use it to sell your product or service, but use it only on people who come to you. They are, so to speak, already in your trap. You have to "bait" the customers who are "running free," but you need no tempting morsels for the ones who are in your "snare."

Here the analogy stops. You don't "skin" your customer, but you don't let him go either! You close the deal and make him glad he walked into your "trap."

22

Lean, Mean, and Hungry Close

When you have just lost a big sale but you've not yet left the building—that's the time for one last try, one more for the road, so to speak. Losing a sale you know you should have made causes terrible frustration. In fact, self-recrimination just rages in you like a fire! "What happened? Why did I lose the sale? What did I do that was wrong? I thought I had it in the bag. I could see myself writing up the sale."

The cynic says there are three things certain in life: death, taxes—and divorce. Some would like to add a fourth: the frustration at losing a sale. For years I accepted defeat grudgingly on this, blaming myself for being inept. Finally, one day I reached the point of absolute desperation. As I mentioned in Chapter 21, I sat in the office of Frank Hasselman of La Haas Corporation of Mendota, Minnesota. He gently told me he wanted to train his people—that he should train his people, but that he wanted to wait until next year. Though the new year was only about seven weeks away, I fumbled around and half-heartedly agreed.

Then, while standing in Frank's parking lot, a rage built up inside me. I walked briskly back to the building. When I arrived at his office, the door was closed. I knocked on the door. Frank said, "Come in." I stood; he sat, and I said: "Frank, you'll gain nothing by waiting seven more weeks. Your people need help right now on communications, goals, human relations, sales—everything!" I said this with a strong conviction and 100 percent sincerity. I told him I was ready to start next Tuesday at 5 P.M., right at his plant. Without a word, Frank stood up, dialed an inside number, and said, "Ernie, we're going to Sheehan's class next week on Tuesday." When I walked out of there, Frank thanked me for my determination.

Incidentally, we had a terrific class with this group. His people improved, and my self-confidence improved even more! As I stood in the parking lot where just minutes before I stared at total failure, I got mad all over again about all the other sales I missed because I did not go back to people who just minutes before had said no. Some call this the "second-effort close." Some call it the "lost-sale close." Others call it the "door knob close." In any case, it's a question of simply making up your mind on one last try for the sale you just missed. You decide on an immediate effort to recapture that big one that just got away. As every fisherman knows, old Grandpa Muskie may be lurking on that fishing reef "just over a piece."

A refinement of the close is to go back again after a miss and ask: "Where did I go wrong here? My product is made for your situation," or "Somehow I must have offended you by my statements, my behavior, my personality. In any event, we both lose. You don't get the benefit of my product, and I lose your business," or "I hope to be in business a good long time and sincerely want to be able to serve you," or "My career is selling. Would you mind telling me where I went wrong?" Count on it; he'll help only if you ask. Many times he'll do the closing himself.

My experience tells me that in three out of four closes, there are external forces that have absolutely nothing to do with the salesman. You sense this from responses your efforts produce.

He might say, "I won't need it for 60 days." So you set up a 60-day delivery date.

"Your product's got a different style from the one I'm used to." Your move here is to place your product with him on a test basis.

"We're conserving cash, and I didn't want to ask you for terms." Give terms if you can.

"Frankly, I was having a bad day; thanks for your courtesy in coming back." Thank him; start over and close!

"I don't have anything in the budget till next month, so I didn't order." Get a modest order with a cancellation privilege written into it.

"Your credit department teed me off with a double billing." Apologize; take notes on his complaint; and close the sale.

With rare exceptions, his put-offs can be answered in such a way that you'll get orders from up to 60 percent of those people from whom you first walked away. You let your hair down; the buyer lets his hair down. You'll be amazed how fast you arrive at a better understanding. There's nothing wrong with a short, straight-faced statement such as: "Where did I fail?" Just take a few minutes to go back and ask: "What did I do that caused you not to order when there is a need for my product?" As soon as you have his answer, the chances are you will know what to do next.

Closing is always on the pro's mind. It's never out of sight. He or she is always closing. More often than not, the prospect admires you for your 100 percent sincerity and

straightforwardness. You're telling the prospect you mean
business; you want the prospect's business; you'll go the extra
mile to help. Louis Hardy of Crockett, Texas, told me in class
one day in Dallas that he was "lean, mean, and hungry," and
that this was his philosophy of doing business.

Why do you get delay after delay in what you'd call
"cinch sales"? Most of the time it's due to overconfidence. You
have to remember that in selling nothing is for sure, absolutely
nothing! So always expect the need to be persistent in closing.
Few, if any, buyers ever leap up in the air with pens poised
and cry "Where do I sign?" A bartender may say: "How about
one for the road, Joe?" but never a buyer.

Be prepared for the obvious put-offs, such as "Give me
your card." (Make sure your card is three times the size of
others. It gets more attention. Mine is gold in color and gets
hundreds of compliments a year.) "See me next week" or "See
me next trip" or "Let me think about it" are other stalls. They
are very human, very normal, and extremely common.
Patiently explain the necessity of purchasing now. Offer test
or trial orders, display orders, stocking orders. Use everything
you can, as pleasantly as you can, at your first meeting.
Expect to make as many as 75 percent of all sales on the first
contact. You may not actually close then, but you sense that
the buyer is solidly pointed in the buying direction. Getting
the details together may take two or more interviews, but
make that first interview count! With the right dress, the right
behavior, the right delivery of your sales talk, and the right
close you will get the right order.

The odds of closing or setting up a closing on the first
interview are all in favor of the true professional. The
unorganized peddler just keeps going back and back.

At this writing, the cost of an industrial sales call in
America is nearly $100. Win, lose, or draw, it is still a
hundred dollars! The big secret is to gear up for more first-

time successes. It means more training, better presentations, and just more professionalism. The peddler may win talk-athons, but the real salesman wins orders.

Even if you are a real pro, you'll walk out of places in your sales career, time and again, with the fatal feeling you've missed something, but you won't drive off into No Man's Land. You will take time to backtrack that prospect to find out where you went wrong. It takes guts to go back. I know, because I do it several times a month! It takes courage; but more than that, it takes conviction that what you sell will truly save or make a buck for the prospect. The true name for the "go-back close" should be the "belief close," because it does take real conviction to return to the scene of a failure and ask for another chance.

"Where did I go wrong here?" "Did I give you a poor sales presentation?" "Don't you like my company?" "Did I offend you?" Only a real "believer" has the humility to ask questions like these.

Sometimes I get: "You're higher, Sheehan, than anyone else in town." I smile; I'm proud of that! I tell them, "I compete with no one but myself." Then I really pour it on to justify my prices. Don't sell features; sell benefits. True selling is not putting something over on someone; it's not stuffing something down his throat. No, I equate selling with friendship. People have paid me more than $5 million in tuition fees simply because I "telegraphed" to them the fact that I was more interested in their success as persons than just in their one-time tuition payment. The commissions, the bonus, the wages that we receive are important, but even more important is our sincere desire to help people through crises, through problems. Show your feelings; don't be in too big a hurry; have empathy for people; demonstrate help-fulness; be alert; keep your promises. Before you know it, you'll grow as a professional salesman. People will rely on you for your judgment. Don't we all trust people who we know want to help us?

In summary, when you honestly feel you deserved the order—that it should have been yours—do these things:

- Briskly walk back to the prospect's door with 100 percent more determination.
- Ask a question. Let your hair down. Say, "Where did I go wrong here? I believe my product will help you."
- Listen, listen, and listen.
- Offer solutions to his problems and ask for the order.
- Do a better job on first interviews; get an "assent close." Be prepared to fight more for business in the all-important first interview.

"How much guts do you have left?" is a good question to ask yourself every day. I do! Do you have the courage of your conviction that people are better off with your product or service, or are you a "half-minder"—someone who is only half sold on his products? Remember what "guts" stands for: "Get You To Sign."

The real question of the hour is whether you'll turn around and fight for what you believe. Incidentally, you never get tired of victory, as General Dwight Eisenhower once said.

Go back again and again, two and three times a week. Soon you'll convert "no sales" to "sales" by your effort and by asking "Where did I go wrong here?" It is so simple, yet so effective.

It just keeps on getting orders for thousands of sales-people all over America. Ours would be a far better profession if we all went back for one more.

This kind of "one more for the road" produces broken records—sales records, that is!

23
162 Closing Tips

1. Start with a close—"Would you like to own this dishwasher?"
2. Ask for a test order: "Try one dozen of these on a test basis."
3. Merely put an "X" on the order blank; point to it with a pen, but say nothing.
4. "Psych" yourself up before a sale so you'll stick in there.
5. Leave the closing situation; give yourself a pep talk; then return and close.
6. Offer a choice: "Do you prefer this one or that one?"
7. The testimonial—"The Miller Company saved 10 percent in fuel on this machine."
8. Trial balloon: start with "if"—or, better—"when you purchase this item."
9. "The Door Knob Caper": act defeated; leave; return; close.
10. Use facts, statistics, examples that close.
11. Have your prospect talk to a satisfied customer on the phone.

12. Look for verbal and physical buying signals: his eyes widen, he touches the merchandise, or says, "I like it."

13. Ask the prospect four or five different times for the order, using different closes each time.

14. Bring a satisfied customer with you on the sale.

15. Cement an order with a small deposit. The layaway plan closes!

16. Allow the prospect to use your product or service for 72 hours (sometimes called "the puppy dog close").

17. Offer a quantity discount.

18. Use the 2 percent cash discount to close.

19. Bring an expert with you.

20. Use demonstrations to close—always best for mechanical items.

21. Offer the "buy one to get one free" deal.

22. Be subtle. Ask: "Do you think you'd be happy with this car?" A positive reaction is your signal to "spring."

23. Use the Ben Franklin Balance Sheet of closing. Use a few negatives to call attention to the many positives. Add, on paper, the benefits he gets. Then have him list on the other side the debits of the deal.

24. Use a minor point: "Will you take the home if drapes are included?"

25. Have the buyer check with the Better Business Bureau on your company.

26. When a buyer criticizes the price, don't defend your product. Sell the benefits to him.

27. Develop your killer instincts in closing. Every customer has a "jugular vein"—his pride, his greed, his comfort.

28. Show no emotion, high or low, until you close.

29. In dealing with women buyers, don't talk down to them. If you can get the floor, don't blow it.

30. Women buyers always have a favorite color. Find it; talk about it.

31. Buyers of the opposite sex have their own radar, so don't flirt. It'll only complicate your close.
32. Almost all buyers, men and women, are offended by body odors. Use deodorant.
33. When the buyer says, "Can I have this or that?" ask: "Will you take it if you can?"
34. Use a silent close. Shut up after you ask a closing question. Even if the prospect says "yes," you won't hear him over the pleasant sound of your own voice.
35. Use special sales and weekly or daily specials to get business.
36. Understand the urgency of the close. You either sell or will be sold.
37. Offer a reduced price. Some buyers hate to pass up a chance for some small "larceny."
38. Don't talk for more than three minutes. Let the buyer talk.
39. When the prospect looks at or picks up an item, remain silent.
40. When the prospect seems to go through temporary insanity—when he gets buyer's remorse, wants to back out of the sale—remain calm.
41. Offer your pen to your prospect when he okays the order.
42. Always ask the prospect to "okay" an order, never to "sign" it.
43. Don't sit all the time; get up and walk around.
44. If a buyer asks for the restroom, follow him—unless, of course, you happen to be "Ms. Salesperson"—or vice versa.
45. Watch the prospect's eyes. When they grow "wide," you are seeing a buying sign.
46. If he says "yes" too often, ask him why he has decided *not* to buy. Too many yeses usually mean a final no.

47. Ask for an add-on order—this item and one of another item.
48. Be relentless. Keep closing.
49. Instructional close: show the prospect how something works.
50. You must dominate the sale or you won't close—don't give him too much sympathy or you'll lose.
51. Don't ask for a close. Just do it.
52. "Executive cooperative close": phone your boss while selling a customer; he'll help close over the phone.
53. The assumptive close: assume the customer will buy.
54. Phone some satisfied customer—a doctor, lawyer, or whatever. Have the prospect talk to him.
55. The negative close: "You're here to buy a house. This is really a big thing. Are you sure you want to buy a house?" The customer will usually turn very positive and buy. He will prove to you that he wants it.
56. "I need to talk it over with my spouse (or banker, or lawyer)" is a statement that calls for this: "If your spouse likes it, are you ready to buy?"
57. You ask: "Are you concerned as to when you will occupy this house?" He says, "Yes, I need it in 30 days." He has closed himself.
58. In nearly 75 percent of the cases, the big-time pro decides, after qualifying, what the prospect will buy.
59. Remember that top closers are healthier, stronger, and nicer. They live longer. They are also more popular—especially at the bank.
60. Top closers must have 110 percent belief in themselves. They won't be denied their closes.
61. Close sales on purpose instead of by accident.
62. A salesman spends only 5 percent of his time on closing, and he's paid in direct proportion to how many closes he gets in that limited time.

63. Keep in mind that in the selling field, you close or you don't get paid.

64. Remember that prospects get real satisfaction out of purchasing.

65. Make the prospect's "jitters" work for you.

66. Listen twice as much as you talk. The prospect must digest what you say. You want him to "swallow the hook," not your words.

67. Closing early is better than closing late.

68. Have seven different ways to ask for the order.

69. You must *expect* to close the sale. Have your pen, scratch paper, order book, brochure. Bring all your tools.

70. People expect you to ask for the order. Ask!

71. "Congratulations on your coming here to own the best ——in the U.S.A." can be used as a greeting close.

72. "What's your favorite color or style?" is a sentence that suggests it's the last thing you need for the order.

73. Prepare eight to ten closing questions. Memorize them; use them.

74. Almost 70 percent of all objections are false, just not true. People lie. "Lie" rhymes with "buy," so pretend he's a "buyer," not a "liar."

75. "I can't afford it" is almost always a stall. The prospect is just not sold on the product.

76. "You said you would buy in 30 days. Okay, let's write up the order now, and date it for then" is a good closing line—or, better, a "close" line on which to hang an order!

77. "If you were my own mother, I would tell you to take it" is a good pitch—but don't use it on a young woman! (But your daughter selling cookies might try the mother line on a young bride.)

78. Switch back and forth, from cost to trade-in, to keep the momentum of the sale going.

79. The picture close: let the prospect use a balance sheet listing "reasons for and against." You give him the "reasons for." Let him find the "reasons against."

80. When the prospect "freezes up," use "the psychology push"—compliment him on something, as in: "I can see you're the kind who doesn't rush into things, but . . ."

81. Put an "X" on the order in the lower right corner. Turn away. If the prospect hasn't signed when you turn back, point to the spot and hand him the pen.

82. When the prospect is right on the cliff, push him gently.

83. Make out the order in advance.

84. Dicker with the prospect. Offer him some choices, but steer him away from the idea that "not buying" is a choice.

85. "You want to help your employees sell more, don't you, sir?" is a question to which your client cannot say no.

86. Pick up the item, give it to the prospect to see, and remain silent.

87. Plan each call so well that it is almost automatic to close.

88. Learn to ask for an order without fear or flubbing.

89. Ask yourself before every call, "What will I say?" Don't be like the green lieutenant who taught gunnery on the day of attack.

90. Ask yourself, "What will I show?"

91. Ask yourself what size of order you'll ask for—small, medium, big?

92. Talk convincingly, economically. You save time and earn closes.

93. Always talk benefits, service, advantages.

94. Bring something to any close; show a few items—photos, samples, or anything that will catch your client's eye. Eighty-seven percent of our impressions come through the eyes. When you talk, only nine percent of it is "seen"—and sometimes even less is heard. (If he is one

of those rarest of people, a good listener, he's already in the bag!)

95. Write a card: "I can save you time, labor, and money."

96. Get the prospect to talk, look, hold, or taste. The "who, what, when, where, how, and why" of the reporter get the readers' attention. You can close your customer the same way.

97. A man or woman who asks questions never argues—he or she usually closes on the answers given.

98. Always write something on paper: the client's profit, costs, discount, interest savings.

99. Teach yourself to listen better. Hear what's being said. Show interest. If you want to bore, talk. If you want to sell, listen! (Pretend it's 3 A.M., and your spouse caught you coming in. You'll listen!)

100. The prospect must believe you. This means you tell the truth today, tomorrow, the day after tomorrow. When you tell the truth, you never have to live in fear.

101. Don't sell four times and buy it back five times. Don't oversell.

102. Control your emotions during the sale. Don't lose your cool. Like steel, good salesmen hold their temper.

103. Fifty hours a week selling should bring outstanding income. Time is a salesman's capital—provided he spends it in closing.

104. Physical fitness helps your closing average.

105. A major cause of fatigue in salesmen is closing failures: failure to plan, failure to organize.

106. Up to 35 percent more closes can be obtained by the salesman who follows a sales interview with a request for additional business.

107. One hour of hard product-study a week—like every Sunday night—will increase your closing percentage at least 5%.

108. There must be a profit for both the buyer and the seller. This great combination is known as "leaving a little bit on the trading table."

109. A pleasant personality helps your closing average. The confidence you get from closing helps your personality, so start a nice circle—the opposite of a vicious circle!

110. Ask for what you want: how much? how many?

111. Before you even make the call, have at least three reasons why the client should buy your product.

112. Look like a person with whom the prospect wants to do business. Smile. Dress right.

113. Capitalize on your strengths. Use what you know.

114. Don't forget that closing is a business—one of the most important jobs in the world. Business profits come not from making things but from selling things.

115. Your face-to-face selling time in a week is very limited—as little as five to eight hours—so you *must be prepared*.

116. As Elmer Wheeler said, "Don't sell the steak, sell the sizzle."

117. Your first 15 words are the most important.

118. Say it with flowers! Use showmanship, smile, change tone, put enthusiasm into your voice!

119. Watch the tone of your voice; keep it soothing. Woo your client.

120. You must sell with enthusiasm. Enthusiasm is really knowledge on fire.

121. You must be sincere and firm when closing.

122. Have a daily hour of self-improvement planned. It's been proven over the last 25 years to be the number-one self-confidence builder. You don't have confidence in a dummy, especially if that dummy is you!

123. Closing sales should become a habit—like shaving every day. (If you prefer a beard, change that to read: "like checking for gray hairs every day.")

124. Review your daily closings. This way you won't lose sight of the good thing you did or said that closed the sale. You may have made one of the many startling discoveries that thinking men make.
125. Resolution, dedication, and willpower will help you close. Self-discipline is a very small price for success. Everything good is the result of sacrifice. If you sacrifice "the extra wink" this morning to keep your 7 A.M. breakfast appointment, you will sleep better that night.
126. Adapt yourself to the buyer. Don't force him to adapt to your style.
127. Buying and selling is not a tug of war. The word "salesmanship" really means "friendship."
128. "See five people per day, tell your story honestly and sincerely, and you'll sell!" says the great Frank Bettger.
129. Service will close more sales than anything else. "He who serves best, profits most."
130. Women are not as mysterious to salesmen who try to understand them.
131. Beat women at their own game. Use charm just as they charm you.
132. Don't ignore wives, husbands, or secretaries; always bring them into the sale. Experts claim approximately 70 percent of all sales made in the United States are made after the nod of a spouse. Without the spouse's support, you could be courting bankruptcy.
133. Women are often more imaginative than men. It's helpful to use colorful language with them to "paint pictures" of what you're saying.
134. To become known as a great closer, try to establish a record. Put yourself in your client's place. Would you rather be called on by a well-known winner than by penny-ante Joe?
135. You'll sell yourself ragged if you listen to prospects who

want you to "come back." Change your state of mind to closing on the first interview. If you decide you've got to do it, you can do it. It's impossible to call back on everyone, so change your attitude and close now.

136. Develop the attitude that you either win or lose on the first interview and that you must win on the first interview.

137. Don't think of the commission you'll gain by selling a prospect, or you'll normally lose. Approach the prospect with the thought of helping, not selling. Think only of what the prospect gains by buying your product. How, in other words, could you possibly let such a nice guy as your client try to get along without your automobile? Remember the Golden Rule!

138. Women buyers are often more interested in the styling, color, and design of a product than are their male counterparts. When you're selling to women, test them on it.

139. "The customer is always right," stated Philadelphia department store owner John Wanamaker. The top closers always make room for, and handle, customers' objections.

140. Women, as a rule, are more conservative than men.

141. Give praise, praise, and more praise to women. This idea of praise is even in the Book of Proverbs: "The woman who is wise is the one to praise" (Proverbs 31:30). To ignore, to talk down to, to belittle, to be insensitive to women is economic suicide—and it could also get you escorted to the door!

142. In selling, especially to women, play on the buyer's vanity with phrases like "Don't you deserve the best?" and "Indulge yourself a little."

143. Women can spot at once men who appreciate and understand them, men who like them for what they are. Don't run down women. They're the other half of

humanity, and, as so many husbands are forced to admit, "the better half."

144. Remember you are in the people business, not the appliance business or the lumber business. In the people business more than half of your customers could be women.

145. Ego-drive closes hundreds of sales every day. Certain people just don't like to lose. Let the sale challenge your pride in your own ability.

146. Always ask: "How long have you been thinking of purchasing a radar range (or whatever)?" The reply should be very revealing.

147. When people call you, get to them at once while they're hot. Just listen and take the order. Don't make a sale, just take the order. Wasn't it the great Civil War general, Nathan Bedford Forrest, who said: "Get there the fustest with the mostest"?

148. A strong, emotional story often helps close a sale. Walt was having family troubles, wife troubles, business troubles. He was just at his wit's end. He was already thinking of bankruptcy; his wife threatened divorce. He took the Don Sheehan Sales Course, and within one year he increased his income 400 percent. As a plus— worth far more than the 400 percent—he and his wife felt that the course experience enabled them to live together and solve their problems. This story is true and has helped me sell many of my courses. You can use stories of this kind to make sales.

149. In selling a certain company, I hit on the statement: "If you like what you see here today, can you make a financial decision on it?" Now if the client says yes, I continue. If he says no, I promptly ask him, "Who can I see who can make a financial decision?" (Resist the temptation to ask: "Well, may I see your wife?")

150. The average cost of a sale today is estimated by some

authorities to be as much as $75 to $100 per call. At that price you cannot afford to be careless! This means you must do a thorough selling job to compensate the high cost of call.

151. If you are in a bad slump, sit down and figure out what each sales interview is worth to you. One man figured he had made 300 sales interviews in a year for an income of $15,000. He figures each interview was worth $50, whether he sold or not. So when you are in a slump, figure out what each call is "worth" to you. Then you will start thinking of how to raise the average by eliminating mistakes. As the dropout said: "If I only had known what I ought to of knew, I'd never of did what I done!"

152. When you make a telephone call, do you know how much it's worth to you in income? Robert Duffy of Minneapolis, Minnesota, told me that each time he dialed, he made $5.12—even if the line was busy or not answered!

153. Don't be afraid to take off a half day or even the whole day just to organize your selling calls.

154. I guarantee that when you stop keeping records of your sales per interview, your volume of sales, and your profit per call, your closing average will plummet, and disaster will strike. You just don't know where you are. Selling then becomes completely haphazard.

155. Any veteran salesman knows he must clearly define his job and analyze his records.

156. Discouragement is mainly the product of idleness. Consistent closing activity chases the blues away.

157. Good accurate sales records will help you avoid slumps. Records will point out your problems. If one of the problems happens to be you, then reread this chapter.

158. "Acres of diamonds" are usually found in your own working area, if you want to find customers.

159. Constantly, daily, prospect. This is the lifeblood of selling. You can't close unless you have a prospect to close. You won't find the "gold in them thar hills" unless you prospect. In other words, prospect or perish.

160. The telephone should be used as a basic selling tool: to get an order, to set up appointments, to obtain reorders, to check customer satisfaction, and to get referrals from your clients.

161. In fighting slumps, make more phone calls and do more looking for new customers. While you are busy, you are doing something to get out of the slump, and it cuts down your worry time.

162. Service your accounts quickly and efficiently; your customers were hard enough to close, so don't open things for your competition. By the way, if it happens to be your wife phoning up a storm, go get your golf clubs—but be ready to catch when she heaves the phone at you.

24
Group Selling—
The Fastest
Way to Sell

"Men were born to succeed, not to fail."
—Henry Thoreau

"And to give group presentations."
—Don Sheehan

Selling to a group of two or more people can multiply your income and your excitement, but you cannot neglect the sales preparation: deciding where the talk will be given and working out the actual talk, the close and follow-up.

You should ask for one hour to give your talk and then hold it down to 45 minutes. A group presentation does many things; it is worth a bit more time.

First, you expose a product or service thoroughly to a number of people and thus save their company—and yourself, of course—a lot of valuable time. In addition, you hurry up the decision process. Everyone in the group participates in a controlled manner and hears a presentation that is good enough to lay the groundwork for emotional appeals and other techniques to shorten the decision-making time.

Your preparation, your environment, your technique, your follow-up all greatly enhance the percentage for making the sale—perhaps from zero to 100 percent! Finally, if you're good at selling to groups, it's one of the fastest ways to get into a five-figure income. I know! You become a professional salesman, a complete salesman, when you can sell to groups.

SHEEHAN'S FIVE-STEP FORMULA FOR GROUP SELLING

1. Decide on your strategy and techniques.
2. Determine how to control the selling environment.
3. Choose the best-known method of presentation.
4. Use a set-up selection sheet to close.
5. Follow up on all your customers.

Step 1. When you talk to a group, remember your audience is made up of people who come to the presentation in a very independent frame of mind. Your first effort should pull the group together with such a well-designed talk that the acceptance of your plan becomes a common cause.

Do not be unduly friendly with those present. Be a little standoffish. My five group presentations per week for 20 years—some 5,000 meetings—have taught me to stay away from the group until I get into my talk. A polite "hello" or "hi" is fine, but don't get long-winded.

Start talking when the top man assures you it's okay. Introduce yourself modestly. Chances are if the boss or group spokesman introduces you, he will end up being negative! He will usually mispronounce your name and offer toned-down, more or less neutral comments: "Mr. Presentor is here today at his insistence for us to hear his plan," or, much worse, "Mr. Presentor thinks his product is better than X's product." It can start you off on a negative basis. It's *your* meeting. You do not in any way want to acknowledge competition.

Step 2. Before you give your presentation, get the environment under control whenever possible. You're much better off if you can get a group on your own ground—your office, your company meeting room, or some hotel or motel of your choice. Use a U-shaped room or classroom with tables to write on. Make sure attendants have paper and pens—but no literature to let the cat out of the bag! Water and glasses should be handy, and coffee should be delivered before the meeting begins.

Thorough preparation is needed to set up a successful meeting. Don't wait until the last minute to assemble equipment, such as blackboards, coat racks, covered tables, a podium, display tables, or tape recorders. You must be equipped and rehearsed to succeed at group selling. Have a detailed list right down to eraser and chalk.

Step 3. Greet your people. Seat them. Start exactly on time. Objects to be shown should be covered by a cloth. Do not show off your product in advance. Basic showmanship dictates that your wares should be camouflaged to create a bit of mystery and stir curiosity in even the toughest buyer. Your presentation should start with 10 to 12 facts and observations written on the blackboard before the seminar begins. These items should be based on the need your participant has for your product or service. The "number presentation" invariably gets your audience at once to crystallize its thinking. I start slowly with an easy smile, introduce myself, and spend three to four minutes "warming up the group" to what it will learn in my brief presentation. I tell them my name is Don Sheehan and I've been working with people for 25 years. "My techniques, my methods," I tell them, "put extra sales on the books for thousands of companies all over the world." In other words, I tell my listeners they'll get something of value from my talk.

I use facts and observations to excite my listeners about my training courses. You possibly can use these or similar facts to sell your product or service. Check to see if everyone has writing materials and then ask your audience to take notes on eight or ten points such as these:

- Ninety-two and one-half percent of companies fail because they are not managed right.
- For every 100 companies that start in business, 75 fail within 48 months.
- Eighty percent of a manager's time is spent trying to unravel yesterday's foul-ups.
- Fifty percent of our managers break down emotionally every year.
- One percent of all companies continuously train their people.
- Fifty percent of the companies that go broke fail because they don't charge enough, not because they charge too much.
- Only one percent of all salespeople make more than $50,000 annually.
- Twenty-five percent of the companies that go broke flop because their help steals them blind.

Your job is to exploit, in a big way, the common problem in the business of the people in your audience. Dig the hole deep and wide. Then *stop!* Yes, stop! Ask each participant—if the group is around five to eight—what point interested them the most. A risk? Yes, but this way you get more participation without burying people in a ton of talk. You can even ask this question of groups of from 10 to 15. Dwell on each point briefly, even on negative factors—then stop. Ask the participants to look at what they've written and to comment on the one point that interested them the most. When a participant speaks, do not interrupt. Let him talk for a minute or two. Occasionally your first speaker will balk and not talk. Act a little annoyed and then go on to the next participant. Always thank each participant. In a big group, ask five or six to express themselves as to what was important to them and ask for the number of the point as listed on their sheets.

After each has spoken, step in with comments on the blackboard or overhead projector and show six to ten solutions that you brought up initially. Show how you can solve problems, save or make money for them. Do it enthusiastically and in a charming way. Really pour it on. Have testimonial letters up front on how your product, your service, will solve their problems—with their good cooperation. Show them they can get their job done if they form the right team—with you and your product or service in the quarterback slot.

Step 4. Here is where most salespeople break down. They don't make a smooth transition into the close. I distribute an orange sheet (8½″ × 11″) that lists various choices. I ask them to select topics that interest them. A copy of my selection sheet is shown in the accompanying figure.

Selection Sheet

Date_____

1. ____ I'm interested in your manager seminars.

2. ____ I'm interested in your sales seminars.

3. ____ I'm interested in your speed-reading seminars.

4. ____ I need to confer with my people more. Call me for an appointment.

5. ____ I need more data on_____.

Name_____ Position_____

Comments_____

_____

_____

So, to take the curse off the close, use a prepared sheet, all printed up. This way you keep your nerve up. Ask participants to put the date on the sheet. Ask them to merely "X" their interest. Ask them to fill in their names. You must stand your ground here. Do not weaken one bit. Stand in front of that group three, five, yes, up to ten minutes, just closing. If it's a public group, ask them to give selection sheets to you at the close of the meeting. Tell them if they do not "X" an item, you will not call them. If it's a company group, ask them to give the sheets to Mr. Big, but keep an eye on the participants as they hand the questionnaires to their boss. Ask if there are any questions. Answer briefly. This is the close. No smiles. Everything business. Stand your ground. Pick up unclaimed selection sheets. Give out extra copies if requested.

Do not hand out any literature! It merely gives them an excuse for not doing anything.

Thank the group. Then pick up your materials, slowly. Deliberately delay your departure by 10 to 15 minutes to invoke questions. Only answer by saying, "When I see you, I'll talk about it." Tell them, in effect, that your answer goes with your product or service. Keep your composure. No more selling. Just close.

Step 5. With a public group you must get back to your audience with a follow-up within 48 to 72 hours while everything is still fresh in mind. As a general rule, only 10 percent are closed outright in a group presentation. The balance, 90 percent, are closed with your follow-up procedure.

Recently in Milwaukee, Wisconsin, I had only six sales at the end of my presentation. By following up on the phone 72 hours later, I ended up with a total of 17 sales—nearly 200 percent. All it took was investing two additional hours in phone follow-up.

In following up by phone, thank the participant for attending the group meeting. Then set up an appointment to continue negotiations. (If you're unsure, don't waste his time and yours.) Ask—after studying his sheet—not *if*, but *when* he'd like to discuss his choice and set up an individual meeting. If he begs for more time, ask him to set up an appointment for you at his office. When you show up for the appointment, don't do any more selling, just concentrate on closing.

The New York Sales Executive Club shows that 50 percent of all American salesmen make two calls and quit. Successful salesmen—about 10 percent of all of them—make five or more attempts. It's this ten percent of the sales force that sells 60 percent of everything that is sold in the United States! So follow up that group talk with a vengeance! You're plenty good if you close one out of three individuals or companies attending your group presentation.

In summary, sell to a group of three or more by using the Sheehan five-step formula:

- Your strategy is to sell a group with an expert presentation. Get your listeners into a single-minded positive attitude in your favor.
- Control the environment by picking your own facilities, your room, your time, your way.
- The right approach is "the figure presentation," based on the participant's lack of what you offer.
- The close is best accomplished by distributing printed selection sheets (with boxes to "X"), unsmilingly standing your ground and then picking up their choices.
- Since only 10 percent of a group will make a decision on the spot, you must follow up on 90 percent of the participants to close 33 percent to 50 percent or more. Seldom do they all agree to do something.

My basic five-step formula has directly and indirectly helped me sell over 100,000 people on my classes and ideas. It does work! It will work for you!

Do not fear to put in 50 to 100 hours of preparation in front of a mirror for your group presentation. People who use the right methods to sell groups invariably sell more. If you dread talking to a group, take the Dale Carnegie Leadership Course in Effective Speaking, the best course in public speaking in America! Then practice your head off and try to give one to five group talks per week forever. Soon you'll be rich. When you get 45 minutes, try to spend the time in this fashion:

5 minutes	Opening
15 minutes	Figure presentation
15 minutes	Solutions
10 minutes	Closing

Now you are ready for the decision to buy or not to buy, which takes zero minutes of your valuable time!

You can double your income—and your enjoyment of life—through group selling!

25
The Bread-and-Butter Account

Closing the established account, weekly or monthly, has many advantages: you get your prices; seldom do customers challenge you when they're used to seeing you on a regular basis; plus you save hundreds of hours of waiting and negotiating. This type of customer is AAA for the salesman. I need this kind of business, and so do you!

Milt Cohen of Cut Price Super Markets allowed me to write orders for the Colgate Company because Milt had "100 percent trust in Sheehan." He knew that every Monday morning I'd be in his store taking inventory and setting up displays, all under his direction. At that time, Ajax Cleanser had its highest consumer acceptance in Milt's territory just outside the city of Detroit. I often felt it was due to his selling the cleanser for 10¢ to build traffic.

THREE WAYS TO UP YOUR WEEKLY OR MONTHLY CLOSES

1. Prove yourself in honesty and sincerity and in any other way you can with the customer.

2. Be consistent. Call at the same time—day and hour—for months or years. Your consistency and character show to the buyer.
3. Keep a book on the customer. Always ask permission to take inventory in the warehouse, the backroom, the shelves. Keep track of how much of each item moves in a week or a month. Become scientific with the customer. Win him to your record keeping and character.

If you sell to department stores, grocery chains, drug store chains, plywood or lumber chains, auto parts replacement wholesalers, or manufacturing plants, you will be welcomed as the man who takes the extra time to take invoices and figure out present stock.

Record keeping takes the guesswork out of selling and sets you up to make what I call the "automatic close." This type of sale is won by the salesman's previous efforts. It is prized by most salesmen yet seldom talked of for fear of competition. By automatic weekly and monthly closing I quadrupled my company's business in two years.

It takes time to get your customer to accept your judgment as to the stock he needs and on that basis to give you weekly or monthly orders when you call at his place of business. Your behavior is important. Be all business, and you'll get all his business.

My figures show I saved two hours a week by developing the nearly automatic close at cut-price stores. That's 100 hours annually! By automatic weekly closes I gained two full selling weeks per year. This enabled me to make history with new selling records.

Think through your customer list and ask yourself these questions:

1. Do I have customers now who thoroughly believe in me?

2. Which customer would I feel safe with in presenting my
   automatic weekly or monthly order and getting his
   cooperation and consent, even on a trial basis?
3. Can I get a half dozen customers on this automatic plan?
   Do they want that kind of service and attention from me?

Do you have the courage to attempt this plan?

Buyers are busy people. Use your best manners with
them. Prove to them that you are the best resource for them,
that you and your factory are of one mind. Have him visit
your factory, have him meet your bosses, keep your promises!
Your buyer is looking for dependability in dealing with you.
Don't disappoint him. Don't purposely overload him. Talk to
his sales clients when asked for help. If he needs help on sales
items, build displays. Work with his plant people, his
superiors. Prove your dependability, again and again, as a
supplier, as a resource, as a factory representative.

Twenty percent of all customers do 80 percent of the
business. A manufacturing company in St. Paul recently
showed me that out of 2,010 customers, 37 gave the company
79.2 percent of its total annual volume. Pick winners. Pick
buyers who will grow. Pick the companies that give you the
volume. Don't live and die with the little guy. Pick customers
who are growing and are doing the job.

In summary, here are the secrets of closing weekly and
monthly:

- Sell the buyer on the "automatic close" with your sincerity,
  character, and trustworthiness.
- Keep records of purchases, inventory, stock movement.
- Perform! Do the things that will endear you to the buyers.
- Work the 20 percent of the customers that do 80 percent of
  the volume. Pick winners!

26
My Daily
Closing Prayer

Give me the courage of Moses to ask for and get the order.

Give me the patience of David to wait out my prospect and get my prices.

Give me the wisdom of Solomon so I'll continue to study selling.

Give me the strength of Samson so I'll stay in shape to put in 10- to 12-hour days selling.

Above and beyond that, anoint me with enthusiasm to keep me set on fire to close every day of my selling life!!

Bibliography

Bettger, Frank. *How I Raised Myself from Failure to Success in Selling.* Englewood Cliffs, N.J.: Prentice-Hall, 1949.

Dane, Les. *Strike It Rich Sales Prospecting.* West Nyack, N.Y.: Parker, 1972.

Gallivan, Robert. *How I Started Earning $50,000 a Year in Sales at the Age of 26.* Englewood Cliffs, N.J.: Prentice-Hall, 1963.

Goldmann, Heinz. *How to Win Customers.* New York: Printers Ink Books, 1957.

Hanan, Mack, James J. Cribbin, and Herman Heiser. *Consultative Selling.* New York: AMACOM, 1973.

Hill, Napoleon. *The Think and Grow Rich Action Pack.* New York: Hawthorne Books, 1972.

O'Farrell, Ralph W. *It Is Easier to Succeed Than to Fail.* New York: Castle Books, 1966.

Paulucci, Jeno F. *How It Was to Make $100,000 in a Hurry.* New York: Grosset & Dunlap, 1967.

Raux, Emille. *Handbook of Successful New Sales Ideas.* New York: Castle Books, n.d.

Roth, Charles. *Handbook of Big Money Selling Strategies.* New York: Castle Books, n.d.

Stone, W. Clement. *The Success System That Never Fails.* Englewood Cliffs, N.J.: Prentice-Hall, 1962.

Index

AMACOM Paperbacks

John Fenton	The A To Z Of Sales Management	$ 7.95	07580
Hank Seiden	Advertising Pure And Simple	$ 7.95	07510
Alice G. Sargent	The Androgynous Manager	$ 8.95	07601
John D. Arnold	The Art Of Decision Making	$ 6.95	07537
Oxenfeldt & Miller & Dickinson	A Basic Approach To Executive Decision Making	$ 7.95	07551
Curtis W. Symonds	Basic Financial Management	$ 7.95	07563
William R. Osgood	Basics Of Successful Business Planning	$ 7.95	07579
Dickens & Dickens	The Black Manager	$10.95	07564
Ken Cooper	Bodybusiness	$ 5.95	07545
Richard R. Conarroe	Bravely, Bravely In Business	$ 3.95	07509
Jones & Trentin	Budgeting	$12.95	07528
Adam Starchild	Building Wealth	$ 7.95	07594
Laura Brill	Business Writing Quick And Easy	$ 5.95	07598
Rinella & Robbins	Career Power	$ 7.95	07586
Andrew H. Souerwine	Career Strategies	$ 7.95	07535
Beverly A. Potter	Changing Performance On The Job	$ 9.95	07613
Donna N. Douglass	Choice And Compromise	$ 8.95	07604
Philip R. Lund	Compelling Selling	$ 5.95	07508
Joseph M. Vles	Computer Basics	$ 6.95	07599
Hart & Schleicher	A Conference And Workshop Planner's Manual	$15.95	07003
Leon Wortman	A Deskbook Of Business Management	$14.95	07571
John D. Drake	Effective Interviewing	$ 8.95	07600
James J. Cribbin	Effective Managerial Leadership	$ 6.95	07504
Eugene J. Benge	Elements Of Modern Management	$ 5.95	07519
Edward N. Rausch	Financial Management For Small Business	$ 7.95	07585
Loren B. Belker	The First-Time Manager	$ 6.95	07588
Whitsett & Yorks	From Management Theory to Business Sense	$17.95	07610
Ronald D. Brown	From Selling To Managing	$ 5.95	07500
Murray L. Weidenbaum	The Future Of Business Regulation	$ 5.95	07533
Craig S. Rice	Getting Good People And Keeping Them	$ 8.95	07614
Charles Hughes	Goal Setting	$ 4.95	07520
Richard E. Byrd	A Guide To Personal Risk Taking	$ 7.95	07505
Charles Margerison	How To Assess Your Managerial Style	$ 6.95	07584
S.H. Simmons	How To Be The Life Of The Podium	$ 8.95	07565
D. German & J. German	How To Find A Job When Jobs Are Hard To Find	$ 7.95	07592
W.H. Krause	How To Get Started As A Manufacturer's Representative	$ 8.95	07574
Sal T. Massimino	How To Master The Art Of Closing Sales	$ 5.95	07593